Experimental Marketing

Experimental Marketing

E J Davis
J Walter Thompson Company Ltd

Nelson

THOMAS NELSON AND SONS LTD
36 Park Street London W1Y 4DE
PO BOX 18123 Nairobi

Thomas Nelson (Australia) Ltd
597 Little Collins Street Melbourne 3000

Thomas Nelson and Sons (Canada) Ltd
81 Curlew Drive Don Mills Ontario

Thomas Nelson (Nigeria) Ltd
PO BOX 336 Apapa Lagos

Thomas Nelson and Sons (South Africa)(Proprietary) Ltd
51 Commissioner Street Johannesburg

First published in Great Britain 1970
Copyright © E J Davis 1970

SBN 17 761101 4

Printed in Great Britain by
Butler & Tanner Ltd Frome and London

Contents

Preface

The target group for whom this book was planned consists largely of ABC_1's, aged twenty and over, predominantly but not exclusively male, and engaged in marketing – in the field, or as brand managers, marketing managers or directors in manufacturing companies, or under a number of titles in advertising agencies.

The book is mainly concerned with the statistical and scientific aspects of marketing experiments, but no prior knowledge of statistics is assumed. Since the conditions surrounding experiments vary widely as to their objectives, it is important for those responsible for them to be informed of the basic principles involved, rather than be presented with check-lists or spuriously simple instructions on 'How to knit your own all-purpose experiment'. Each and every experiment in the market-place calls for considerable thought on how it should be organized, controlled, measured and interpreted if maximum benefit is to be obtained from the costs and effort involved. The object of this book is to provide the necessary basis for this approach.

In some cases, perhaps most of all in Chapter 3 in the discussion of when to use test-launching, the argument covers methods and techniques which many companies may find difficult to apply because data for the calculations may not be immediately available. In practice, however, I have found that even where the amount of data has been minimal, the approach has still been useful as a means of putting the available data into a proper perspective and as a background for disciplined thinking leading to rational conclusions.

The examples and applications described are set in markets for consumable goods, where there has been most development of experimentation. The principles, however, equally apply to experiments with consumer durables or industrial products, and given the necessary resources there is no reason why valid and profitable experimentation should not develop rapidly in these areas as well. The examples also tend to be mainly descriptions of failures – in planning, measurement, control, or interpretation – but this is merely because failures are much more instructive than successes. Successes abound in which companies have gained considerably through test launching or market testing, but success is usually specific and has little instructional value outside the particular context in which it was achieved.

My thanks are due to a large number of people with whom I have been able to discuss marketing experiments, but particularly to Dr John Treasure of JWT who first introduced me to the art and mystery of test marketing and who has given me a great deal of encouragement and support ever since. In the final preparation of this book I have been greatly helped by John Downham of Unilever, Paul Gerhold of the Advertising Research Foundation, Bill Weilbacher of JWT New York, Professor Gordon Wills of Bradford University, Malcolm Fry of Ashridge Management College and Tom Corlett of JWT London, who all found time to read scripts and to make valuable comments. Needless to say, any remaining bias, error, or omission is entirely my fault.

Finally my thanks go to Miss June Hurndall, my secretary, who has cheerfully typed and retyped the script in addition to her normal work.

E. JOHN DAVIS

Introduction

Test marketing is one of the most controversial subjects in the field of marketing generally, and has been so for a long time. Other topics may steal the limelight for a while, new marketing methods or research techniques may for the moment become the centre of discussion, but sooner or later some editor or author returns to the theme of 'What is wrong with test marketing?' and controversy revives. At one extreme there are those who simply do not believe in test marketing; at the other, there are companies who appear to spend profitable months or years in experimenting with new ideas or new products so as to get them 'right' before any wide-scale introduction.

What is the lure that marketing experiments possess when, having been criticized and battered from all quarters over the years, and apparently discredited for all time by Gold* in 1964, more experiments are being undertaken today than ever before? Perhaps it is simply because experiments still provide the only logical way by which the risks to be found in many areas of marketing can be effectively reduced.

Gold took area sales data for a number of products, and showed that attempts to estimate national sales volumes by multiplying area sales by various factors gave results with wide ranges of error. This caused considerable comment and discussion both in the United States and in Britain. If results like these could be obtained with established brands under relatively stable conditions, there appeared to be little hope of getting accurate predictions with new brands introduced experimentally into small areas.

One surprising thing about Gold's paper was the reaction to it. People who had for years been paying large sums to research companies, so as to be able to study differences between areas in established markets, suddenly seemed to become aware that area differences could affect experimental results. Typical areas, containing the right proportions of the population in each age group, or social class, or whatever, might not be typical in their appetite for some new product. A test area brand share of x per cent might not in fact indicate a comparable wider market share.

* See Further Reading, page 183.

To those who did not believe in test marketing, the paper gave new ammunition. To those faced with the problem of whether or not to commit themselves widely to costly, but speculative, projects, in the hope of profits but with the risks of losses, there were still no other choices than those of launching, abandoning, or testing. Probably, many of them now became more aware of some of the problems and consequently approached testing with a healthier critical sense than before, but testing still remained the only way to minimize the risk facing them.

Risk stems from ignorance. It may be a highly informed ignorance, as when a company has mapped all the possible outcomes of a proposed course of action but still lacks the vital knowledge to show which outcome is the most probable, or it can be blind ignorance. In either case, a well-directed, well-conducted, and adequately measured experiment, even an experiment that falls far short of the best criteria, will almost inevitably produce some additional information to aid in the processes of formulating a decision.

Experiments can be regarded in a number of ways. They are a powerful method of obtaining experience and information – and whatever the specific information being sought may be, the opportunity should always be taken to examine and investigate as many aspects of the situation as possible. However one defines an experiment, it is not in itself a decision-making process, but only an aid – often indispensable – to that process. Prediction of the wider market effects of a project is by no means the only useful information to be gleaned from an experiment – though too often it is still the only measure sought or considered. Deeper analysis beyond the averages and the percentages of store or consumer audits or surveys will not only provide information to supplement or improve any predictions, but may also indicate ways in which the marketing operation itself may be improved before being carried into a wider area.

At the very least, experiments provide an insurance against disaster, but this is too limited and negative a view. Experiments are also a means of discovery, and those who experiment most often and most usefully will add to their knowledge and become able to improve the efficiency of their operations in marketing, just as the use of these same experimental techniques has improved the efficiency of operations in many other areas.

This has been achieved by using experiments in their proper role, so as to gain experience, information, and understanding – and not by expecting them to operate on a purely mechanical 'accept-reject' basis.

I

Experimental launching and market testing

Experimental marketing is a subject that covers the entire range of situations involved when a company first decides to introduce changes into a small part of its market so as to gain information before becoming committed to innovation on a wider scale.

The changes may be made on a major scale, as at the launch of a new product with all its associated marketing elements or the relaunch of an existing product involving major changes in its presentation and promotion. In other experiments, however, only a single factor associated with an existing product, such as the campaign, the price, or the level of the appropriation, may be changed; or an innovation like a new pack, the use of a new medium, or of a new type of promotion may be introduced. Between these two extremes, experiments may be concerned with assessing the effects of changing two or more factors simultaneously to discover the extent of any interaction between them that could lead to a greater variation in total response to joint variations than the response to varying either one of them singly would indicate.

'A small part of a market' may range from one or two selected stores, through shopping centres or clusters of streets of various sizes, to the whole area covered by a local newspaper or television station. In some instances, the growing internationalization of markets has led to a whole country being used for experimental purposes, either as part of a continental market, as in the Far East, or because conditions in it are similar in certain respects to those in a separate larger market – e.g. Sweden and the United States.

The information sought is normally quantitative, and is obtained from the analysis of factory sales or store or consumer panels, from questioning appropriate samples of people, or through some form of direct observation. In many cases, information is needed only on how some specific change will perform in the market, or whether a required minimum effect is being achieved. In others, a comparative assessment may be required to indicate which of two or more potential courses of action is likely to be the most beneficial.

The precise nature of the data required, and the degree of accuracy necessary in measurements, will vary considerably with the objectives of the experiment. If a new product is involved, with heavy investment in new plant depending on the interpretation of the results, then clearly the results should be measured in as many ways as possible, and with a high degree of precision. The requirements will be as complex when the objective is to provide a basis for a critical decision between alternative courses of action, but at the other end of the scale many experiments require only a few simple measurements. The extreme situation occurs in feasibility testing, where, for example, a small quantity of an imported product or a prototype display stand may be placed in a single store merely to assess whether the item shows enough promise to be worth testing on a larger scale.

Definitions

The whole field of experimental marketing is so wide that some segmentation and labelling of the main parts is useful. The term *test marketing* was originally quite specific, involving putting a new product into a town and observing the results through a store audit. Since those early days, well before World War II, an increasing number of forms of marketing experiment have developed, but unfortunately without any corresponding, or generally accepted, development in nomenclature. Today it is quite common to find the term test marketing used to cover a wide range of these activities, with some consequent risk of confusion and waste.

Figure 1.1

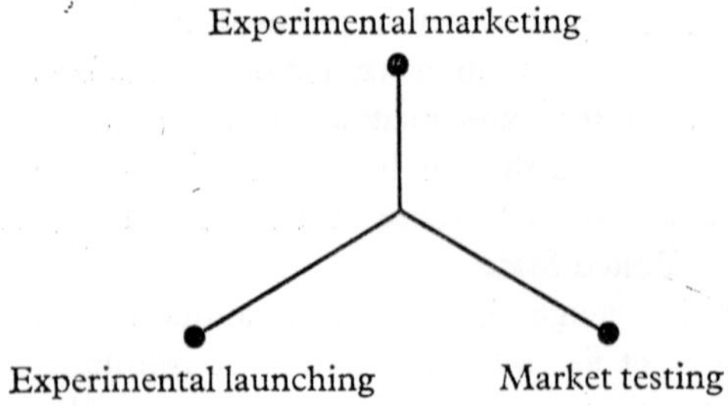

Within the confines of this book at least, the whole area will be divided into a number of parts and given separate names. The first obvious division is between those experiments in which a new product, or a distinctly 'new improved' product, is involved, and those in which variations are being made only to some part of the marketing mix of an existing product. For experiments in the first category, the terms *experimental launch* or *test launch* appear unambiguous and appropriate, while the term *market test* is used for experiments in the latter category (see Figure 1.1).

A second form of the classification of experiments depends on their objectives. Some are undertaken specifically to develop a projection of what is likely to happen if experimental factors are introduced into a wider market, and the label 'projectable' should then be firmly applied to them so that this aspect of the operation becomes firmly fixed in everyone's mind. Others are undertaken with less exacting objectives, as with feasibility studies that are merely meant to assess whether some item has any future at all, or with experiments undertaken to gain general experience or to provide an opportunity to remedy any defects or problems on a small scale before becoming committed to a wider operation.

Projectable test launching

The *projectable test launch* is the most demanding of all types of experimental marketing, and it is also the one in which the stakes are highest, in terms of either profits or careers. In some cases the object of the projections is to determine whether or not sales in the wider market are likely to exceed a specified figure, the whole operation being basically a 'go, no-go' test of the proposed product and marketing plan. More commonly today, with the long lead-times necessary to develop and build new plant, the basic decision to 'go' will have been taken either before or very early during the projectable test launch, the object of the projection being to provide a more refined estimate of likely future sales for use in detailed planning and budgeting. Whichever situation prevails, the major factor distinguishing this type of experimental launch is that projections will be required at the end and full provision must be made at all times to ensure their validity. This demands a rigorously controlled experiment at all stages, together with adequate measurements of sufficient accuracy to provide the data necessary for the projections.

Pilot launching

The other form of experimental launch is the *pilot launch*, where information is being sought for more general purposes. The term is introduced through analogy with the establishment and operation on the production side of a 'pilot plant', between the laboratory preparation of samples of the new product and investment in a full-scale manufacturing facility. In operating a pilot plant there are possibly three basic objectives: (a) to ensure that the proposed method of manufacture will work outside the laboratory; (b) to get any bugs out of the system, or to deal with any problems on a small scale before they can interfere with large-scale operations; and (c) to provide data that will assist in operating the main plant as efficiently as possible.

These same objectives can be broadly applied to pilot launching a new product. Pilot plants and pilot launches often go together, with the main decision to produce and launch having already been taken and with the pilot plant producing a small volume of output which can usefully supply a limited area of the proposed market. A full projectable test launch may be mounted under these circumstances, the full marketing programme being put into the area concerned, but alternatively a more flexible approach in which the marketing plan may be varied as the experiment proceeds may be used in an effort to eradicate any weaknesses or to try alternative methods. This may prove particularly useful in situations where a company is entering a market in which it has no previous experience, and it also offers an opportunity for testing the mechanics of the operation from the way the outers stand up to handling to the efficiency of arrangements for invoicing.

It must be remembered that, if changes are made to the marketing plan during the course of an experimental launch, it may no longer remain possible to generate projections to a wider market since the experiment will then have been conducted under mixed conditions. But there are certainly cases where there may be a greater potential value in taking an opportunity to improve the marketing plan or the mechanical aspects of the venture before the wider launch than in using the facilities so as to provide an excellent projection of a plan that is suffering from weaknesses or deficiencies. The danger is that at the end of the operation it may be difficult to prevent projections being made from a pilot launch which may be very insecurely based if the conditions under which the results were generated have not been rigorously controlled throughout.

Apart from experiments planned specifically as projectable or pilot launches, every opportunity should be taken during area or rolling launches, where a product is launched in one area after another, across a market, to gather from each area in turn data that can be used for more refined projections into other areas; or alternatively to use the early operations effectively as pilot launches to improve the marketing plan.

Market testing

The whole area of market testing can be broken down into a number of categories, depending on the subject of the experiment, i.e. whether it is the product itself, the pack, the campaign, the appropriation, promotions, prices, trade terms, or whatever it may be that is involved. This is not, however, a very useful method of division, as two or more factors can be involved in many of the more sophisticated experiments, and the descriptions become cumbersome.

Market tests generally fall into the projectable category, either because assessments are required of the effects of adopting a single proposed course of action, or because a decision is needed on which of two or more possible alternative courses of action will be the most beneficial. Hence, while pilot-type operations may have their place in this area, the discussion will assume throughout that market tests need to be projectable.

Specific and exploratory experiments

One possible line of division in the market-testing area, and which may become more important with time, lies between specific tests and exploratory tests. In specific tests, whether single or comparative, the

Figure 1.2

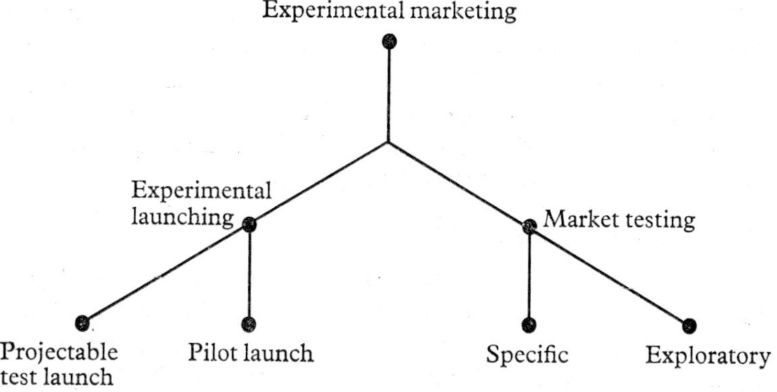

object of the operation is to determine whether or not it will be beneficial to move some factor in the marketing mix to a specified new level, e.g. an appropriation level of £500,000 a year or a new price of £0·15. In exploratory experiments, the objective is to determine the relationship between profits or sales and the experimental factors in the marketing mix, with a view not only to assessing the current optimum level of operation for these factors, but also to provide a tool that will be generally useful for future calculations. Thus the results of experiments are being used to develop mathematical models of parts of the market which illustrate, or even define, the ways in which changes in the various factors in the marketing mix can be expected to operate on the final profit, either singly or as the result of interactions between them (see Figure 1.2).

Exploratory experiments can only be carried out on those parts of the marketing mix which are 'variable', in other words, those that can be measured on some sort of scale – generally money. Other parts of the mix cannot be varied; they can only be changed in some way, as the pack or advertising copy, and although some changes may be more marked than others, there is no numerical scale along which they can be spaced. Experiments with such factors are therefore always specific and likely to remain so for some time yet.

The division between specific and exploratory experiments may prove important in practice. Specific experiments often fail to show conclusive results because the extent of the difference between new and existing situations is too small to be measured accurately within a reasonable budget or with existing methods. With exploratory experiments, however, the factors can sometimes be varied to an exaggerated extent to ensure that a change large enough to be measured will be produced, though without going so far as seriously to impair the validity of any relationship established. At present most market testing falls into the first category, but many specific experiments could with only a modest increase in the budget be turned into exploratory experiments, and with results that would go much farther in illuminating those problems with which the company is trying to deal.

Projections and forecasts

In all forms of projectable experiments, whether they involve a launch or a change in an existing marketing mix, the main interest lies in the projections and the forecasts developed from the area results rather than in the area results themselves. This is generally appreciated in projectable test launches and market tests involving only one variant, but it often appears to be overlooked in comparative tests of two or more alternatives where comparisons almost invariably tend to be made between the area results themselves and not between projections and forecasts based on them.

One reason for this may be that while, with the help of a number of assumptions, it is possible to assess the limits of error in experimental results and thus to decide whether any observed differences are significant – or whether they may be due only to chance movements – assessments of the statistical significance of differences between anything other than simple projections are often impossible. For that reason later discussion on the assessment of the reliability of results is in this book limited to the experimental results themselves.

A second reason is that while only simple methods of projection are used – such as projecting sales per head or changes in brand share – any differences between the projected figures remain so dependent on observed differences between area figures that it does not matter which set is used for comparison. If, however, more sophisticated methods of arriving at projections and forecasts are developed and used – more complex relationships between the experimental areas and the wider market than merely population being incorporated – it becomes quite possible for the smaller of two changes observed in different areas to lead to the larger projected or forecast change in the wider market. This is not as illogical as may appear, and the only safeguard against being misled is to make final assessments and decisions only on the basis of fully developed projections and forecasts at the wider market level.

The need for adequate measurement

Some experiments in the past have failed to fulfil their purpose because the measurements made have not been adequate for the type of projection needed. Some years ago, a new brand of leisure product was marketed in a single television area on an experimental basis. A competitor already carrying out research in the area measured the level of sales and estimated that the new brand might achieve 5 per cent of the national market – a level adjudged too low to make national launching profitable. But in due course, the new brand was launched nationally, took around 5 per cent of the market for a couple of years, and was then withdrawn. The interesting question then arose of why or how the product came to be launched after a test launch from which a correct forecast of failure at 5 per cent of the market was obtainable.

Piecing together scraps of evidence, it appears that while sales achieved by the new brand were certainly properly measured in the experimental area, in order to keep down costs no measures were taken of competitive sales. Thus no measure of brand share was made available, but only a measure of absolute sales, which was grossed up on a population basis to a national level. The resulting figure came to about 15 per cent of estimated national sales, and so seemed adequate to justify a national launch. The company was apparently not aware that, for various reasons, the sales for this type of product were three times as high per head of population in the experimental area than in the country as a whole. Hence, in grossing up to a national level, they reached a figure some three times higher than justified. Then, by failing to discover that they had achieved only 5 per cent of market share in the test, they deprived themselves of the means of making an alternative forecast based on brand shares, which would at least have shown them certain factors that they had not previously taken into account. The outcome of the operation was that while the company had clearly mounted a successful experiment – one from which forecasts were made by others and which were subsequently validated in the national market – they themselves reached wrong conclusions and took a wrong decision because their measurements were not adequate. The amount saved by not measuring competitive brands could not have been more than £1,000, but the losses subsequently incurred have been put at around £250,000.

Variables

Experiments in marketing generally rest on the same body of principles as do experiments in the sciences, in agriculture, biology, medicine, or other similar areas. In each of these areas there are differences in the conditions under which the principles are operated or applied and which make some areas easier than others to work in. Probably marketing is one of the most difficult areas in which to carry out successful experiments, but the principles still apply and can be ignored only at the risk of obtaining misleading results.

In any experimental situations, whether in a laboratory or market, there are likely to be three sets of factors – usually called variables – to be taken into account. These are the dependent variables, the independent variables, and the exogenous variables.

The *dependent variables* are those to be measured in assessing the outcome of the experiment. In most marketing experiments this will include some measure of sales obtained from analyses of factory shipments, store audits, or some form of consumer panel. In others, the level of awareness of a product or campaign, the extent of trial or repeat purchase of a product, the level of distribution in stores, or whatever else may be the appropriate measure of the effect of the experimental changes, becomes a dependent variable. In many experiments, and particularly in those involving launches, measurements should be made on a number of dependent variables in the expected sequence of events, so that if the sequence breaks down, and the expected level of sales is not achieved, then the point of breakdown can be determined.

The *independent variables* are those that are the subject of the experiment, ranging from each component of the marketing mix and the new product itself in an experimental launch to just one single variable in a simple market test. These independent variables must be controlled at the levels at which the experiment is designed to operate, and they clearly cannot be allowed to deviate from these levels without serious risk of the whole operation being invalidated.

The *exogenous variables* are all those remaining factors that may have an effect on the dependent variables, but that are not themselves being manipulated during the experiment. Since a wide range of factors could, under certain conditions, have such an effect, it is wise to regard all other variables, however remote, as being in this category. Some of these variables may be under the control of the company concerned, including, for example, advertising for other brands sold by the company. In the main, however, the exogenous variables – ranging from competitive advertising or the activities of a competitor's sales force, to the prosperity of local industries in the experimental areas or even the weather – are outside the control of those conducting the experiment.

Control areas

To separate those movements in the dependent variables due to the progress of the experiment from those that result from the influence of the exogenous variables, a control experiment must be undertaken alongside the experiment itself. Here the same dependent variables are measured in an area from which the experimental action is excluded, and so any movements can be taken as a measure of the effects of the exogenous variables during the duration of the experiment. Changes due to the exogenous variables alone are therefore measured in the control area, while changes due to the exogenous variables and the independent variables are measured in the experimental area, and so theoretically any difference can be attributed to the experiment.

The same types of variable occur in all other forms of experimentation. In laboratory experiments it is generally easier to enumerate and control the exogenous variables, but even there a well-conducted experiment will be run with a control alongside to ensure that the observed results can be properly attributed to the influence of the independent variables and do not arise from such other conditions as contamination. In agricultural or biological experiments, the exogenous factors are often less amenable to control, and using control samples or control plots is standard practice. The great advantage enjoyed by workers in these areas is not that they have fewer exogenous variables to contend with, but that, through being able to replicate each experiment and control many times over, they are better able to differentiate between their effects and the experimental effects that they are attempting to measure or define.

Unfortunately it is too often the case that marketing experiments are conducted without any corresponding control operations, or else the experiment and control are each conducted only in a single area. If no control operation has been set up, and the assessment of the effects of the experiment is based solely on the differences in the dependent variable before and after the experimental treatment, then there is no way of differentiating between those changes due to the experimental treatment and those that have arisen from the effects of the exogenous variables. Hence the results will be difficult to interpret and may, on occasion, be dangerously misleading.

The assumption that any variations in the behaviour of the dependent variable between experimental and control areas can be attributed to the effects of the experimental treatment, rests on the further assumption that the exogenous variables have affected the readings equally in experimental and control areas. This may or may not be so, but clearly the risk of the assumptions breaking down is likely to be high if only one reading of each type is available for comparison. Such a risk can be reduced only by the replication of both the experiment and the control operations in further areas; in simple terms, the effects due to the exogenous variables are more likely to be averaged out over two series of readings.

Multi-area testing

Unfortunately, the complexity of many marketing experiments, experimental launches in particular, precludes their being mounted in more than a single area. In other cases, limited budgets or some other constraints on the freedom of the experimenter will also confine the operation to a single area. With these cases, therefore, the opportunity for using multi-area experimental designs, in which the effects of the exogenous variables can be properly analysed, may not occur. Even so, there have been numerous occasions when multi-area experiments would have been possible without the operations becoming unduly complex or costly, but where the opportunity was not taken.

Discussion of a project at an early stage often leads to a change of plan and the adoption of a multi-area design for an experiment originally conceived as a single-area test. The risks of single-area testing often remain hidden, particularly when an apparently satisfactory gap is opened between experimental area results and those from the control area, but the dangers can often be demonstrated quite clearly when the results of multi-area experiments are examined.

In one example a new campaign was to be tested to assess whether it could produce any measurable effect on the level of sales in a competitive market. The control areas were to have the latest versions of the existing campaign. Seven television areas were selected for the operation, three being exposed to the experimental campaign and four being left with the existing one. At the end of six months, the results showed upward movements in sales in the three experimental areas, virtually no movement in two of the control areas, a small rise in the third, and a large rise in the fourth that was equal to the largest movement in the experimental areas and greater than the other two. This last result was unexpected, and nothing in the history of the area suggested an explanation. Further investigation showed that a change of a very minor nature had taken place on the sales side of the company organization, but while it had affected this one area quite considerably, it had not affected any of the others. There followed an intensive examination of conditions in all the other areas, but nothing could be identified there that would have affected the measurements unduly.

As a result of these inquiries, the seventh suspect area was dropped from the analysis. While this result had been included, there was a fair indication that the new campaign would be beneficial, but once it was removed, no doubt remained about the outcome of the experiment. Subsequent results from the use of the campaign nationally confirm the validity of the final interpretation. Yet the disturbing thing was that this seventh area could only be identified as being suspect in comparison with the other six, since otherwise it was an admirable area for experimental or control purposes. If just one single experimental area and one single control had been used, drawn from the seven areas, then there would have been one chance in seven of this area being the control and leading to a conclusion that the experimental campaign was less efficient or at most only equal to the existing one, depending on which other area it was paired with. A single area test would have had a 14 per cent chance of leading to the wrong result built into it from the beginning, and without any real indication of the risk involved. Calculation of the 95 per cent limits considered in Chapter 9 would clearly have become an academic exercise.

The greater part of the science, art, and mystery of successful experimentation lies therefore in establishing conditions in which the effects of the independent variables can be separated from the effects of the exogenous variables not amenable to control, so that the true effects of the experimental treatment can be measured. This can be done with a high degree of certainty only in multi-area experiments.

But this is not to say that simple experiments in single areas cannot work at all, though they must inevitably be recognized as less efficient and less reliable. Larger movements in the dependent variables are needed before even the existence of an effect can be accepted. The safeguards that statisticians have built into more sophisticated forms of experimental design against the effects of the exogenous variables being mistaken for experimental effects, are lacking, and this must lead to a loss of precision and reliability.

The costs of experiments

One final point remains to be covered in this introductory discussion. Whatever category an experiment falls into, and whether or not it involves a launch or a change associated with an existing product, the whole purpose of the experiment is to 'buy' experience to meet a specific need. The costs involved are made up in part of the expenses in mounting and measuring the experiment, but where a major decision depends on the results, additional costs arising from delays in reaching an advantageous decision while the experiment is in progress frequently occur. If the launch of a successful product is held back or a beneficial price increase or some other profitable action is delayed while an experiment takes place, the cost of gaining the information is increased by the amount of the profits foregone during the experimental period – either directly, or indirectly through any loss of lead-time. Consequently, testing and experimenting should never be routine. Each situation must be assessed on its merits, with due regard to the market conditions, the probabilities of success and failure, the sums at risk as profits or losses, and the real costs of buying more information through experiments.

While some companies may be criticized for having taken important decisions without sufficient information, there are others who are perhaps more deserving of criticism who take a misplaced pride in never making a major decision without testing. 'Go, no-go' experiments, and particularly those associated with new products, should only be undertaken as a last resort after all other means of reaching a decision have been exhausted and when the risks remaining in the venture are still too great to be accepted as they stand. In these circumstances, the budget and other facilities made available for the experiment should be commensurate with the need for precision in the results.

Conversely, every opportunity should be taken, within or alongside a company's normal marketing operations, to mount exploratory experiments that will lead to a better understanding of the company's markets and the factors which affect them. This is often more a matter of recognizing opportunities, adapting existing conditions, and using existing research measurements than it is of spending large sums on new projects, but the long-term benefits from determining how best to balance the numerous parts of a marketing mix more efficiently in any situation can be considerable.

2

Experimental discipline

The main problem in most forms of experimental marketing is to establish and control a properly organized experimental situation, and unless this is done the whole operation can become not only worthless but also a source of completely misleading information.

Objectives

It cannot be stressed too often that the general objectives of experimental marketing are the collection of unbiased, objective results obtained under specified conditions. This calls for the application, so far as is possible, of proper experimental designs in setting up the situations and for experimental discipline in the control of experiments. Emphasis must be placed on this, first, because those normally responsible for organizing and administering marketing experiments are not usually scientists with a background of experimental discipline, and secondly because they are mostly to some extent involved with the outcome of their experiments. Thus the field of experimental marketing generally, and the area of test launching in particular, tends to become a battleground between the highly motivated approach of the marketing man and the cold detachment of the scientist.

In a marketing context, starting with the proviso that the general objective is to set up in a small area the conditions which would hold for a wider operation of the same nature, then all that experimental discipline calls for is seeing that this is done, no more and no less. In every situation connected with a marketing experiment, the question has to be raised and answered of whether or not a proposed course of action is one that would be admissible within the framework of the proposed national operation, and if it is not, then it should if at all possible be avoided.

Personal involvement

It is probably axiomatic that no one should be expected or allowed to control any marketing operation, or even to take part in one, unless he has faith in the product concerned and in the organization behind it. This clearly should not be a blind faith, but a rational, confirmed confidence based on an assessment and reassessment of the situation and built up through proper consideration of all the available evidence and the results of an appropriate pretesting programme.

Apart from this, there will almost always be at least some measure of personal involvement. At the higher levels, management will have given backing to the product or to the innovation being considered at each stage in its development, besides becoming increasingly conscious at each stage of the amount of resources already invested and of the number of alternative courses of action that have been rejected and that may no longer remain open as options. Furthermore, as time passes and a project comes nearer and nearer to the marketing stage, it will have behind it an increasing number of decisions in its favour that will be open to criticism if management later abandons it or if it fails. In many cases, individual career prospects will at least be thought of as being linked with seeing the project developed to a successful conclusion.

Lower down the line, at the level of area sales managers and representatives, involvement in the project only comes at a later stage, when the experiment is put into the market, but for all that it may be no less intense. Representatives in a test area will know that they are involved in an experimental situation even if their superiors do manage to keep a tight rein on exhortations to produce the greatest possible effort to make the venture a success. Those in the field will at least to some extent be aware that the eyes of management are on the experiment's progress, which will probably mean that daily sales, weekly reports, and other manifestations of their activity are under constant scrutiny. Thus they will soon tend to feel that it is they who are on test at least as much as the experimental activity, and will react accordingly.

Experimental conditions

Now, the object of most experimental marketing activity is either to find out what will happen, or whether certain minimum effects will be achieved, when a change is introduced into the market under normal conditions. The change may be a new product, an increased advertising appropriation, an alteration in price, or whatever, and the normal conditions will inevitably include the enthusiasm which may be induced into the marketing team when such changes are made on a national basis. Experimental discipline demands that in the areas covered by the test the change be introduced under these 'normal' conditions, nothing more and nothing less, so that when assessments are made of the performance of the experiment with a view to estimating the national effect, the results are based on an appropriate expenditure of effort.

With test launches it is extremely difficult, if not impossible, to reproduce in a local area precisely the conditions which would apply there during a national launch – and for this reason some say that it is not worth trying. If, however, test launching or any other form of experimental marketing from which quantifiable results are sought is to be undertaken at all, the fact that it is difficult to reproduce the right conditions must be accepted from the beginning. The difficulty merely makes it all the more important that the demands of experimental discipline should be properly appreciated by those responsible for the conduct of the experiment, and the closest possible approach to normality is achieved.

The demands of experimental discipline can usually be met quite easily so far as the physical factors involved in the test are concerned. In test launching, the product can be made to conform to that which will be marketed nationally, though there may be difficulties on some occasions, as, for example, when an imported product is being used for testing but when domestic production facilities would be set up for national marketing. In some cases where imported products have been used, only the address on the label has been different, but in other cases the subsequent use of raw materials obtained from different sources has led to differences in the characteristics of the product itself. Similar differences in characteristics can arise if, as may happen, the test area is supplied from the production of a pilot plant operating on a reduced scale, and which may lead to some variation in the taste, texture, colour, and so forth, of the product. In all these situations it may be impossible to modify the abnormal factor, and thus flaws begin to appear in the ideal normal construction of the experimental conditions.

Other physical factors, such as prices, both to the trade and to the consumer, are generally more amenable to discipline. The weight of advertising and the media schedules to be employed may present more difficulty, and these will be discussed at greater length in Chapter 11. The content of advertising is usually amenable to control, since the proposed campaigns will normally be used in testing, though there may be difficulties if there have to be changes from a proposed national medium to the best local equivalent if it is one which cannot accept the same matter, e.g. when using black and white in local newspapers, or perhaps posters, whereas the national campaign would use colour in magazines.

Departures from the ideal

Inevitably in many experimental situations, and particularly in those involving test launching of one kind or another where there are a number of physical factors to be considered, there will be some discrepancies between the test situation and the larger subsequent marketing operation. Experimental discipline can accept this situation within reasonable limits, otherwise very little testing would be completed successfully. However, it is very necessary that the whole plan for the experiment should be carefully scrutinized for such discrepancies, and that they should be noted down as and when they become necessary: first to ensure that successive decisions are made in the light of all that has gone before, and of other discrepancies to which the plan is already committed; and secondly so that at all times through to the final assessment the record is available and can preferably be incorporated into all the intermediate and final reports on the operation. Only in this way can it be ensured that the corporate memory of compromises agreed at various stages is brought to bear on the final decisions.

The sales force

For two reasons, more difficult problems arise in maintaining experimental discipline as soon as human factors are involved. First, it is impossible to determine what should be regarded as a normal level of activity in many cases. Secondly, even if it is possible to do this, it is still difficult for those involved in the test to assess whether or not the norm is being achieved or exceeded. Thus, while it is reasonable to expect an all-out effort from representatives in a national launch, it is highly likely that for the reasons already mentioned the representatives involved in a test launch will produce an even greater effort. Neither is this phenomenon confined to the representatives; it can also appear in other levels of the marketing team.

One solution that has been offered to combat the problem of the nvolvement of representatives is contracting the selling operation out to a neutral sales force, who will treat the product merely as one of the many they handle. While there may occur situations in which this would be acceptable, it would appear to be at least as likely to set up an equally atypical set of conditions in the opposite direction. Among these will be the fact that retailers and wholesalers who may have been dealing with the manufacturer for many years, and who may be on close terms with their usual representatives, will suddenly be offered the manufacturer's product – whether a new one in some form of test launch or an old one being sold-in in connection with some other marketing experiment – by a stranger from a different organization. Under these circumstances, reactions from traders are likely to be atypical to some extent, and while the nature of the atypicality may be so apparent that the experiment is obviously jeopardized, it may be more hidden and less easy to assess either in direction or extent.

Using an outside sales force will tend, in practice, to remove not only any excess of zeal associated with the experiment, but also the normal level of involvement which ought to be felt by any conscientious representative engaged in selling his company's products. The bath water goes out with the baby, and the bath water is a very logical and necessary ingredient of the test – if it is at the right temperature. Consequently it is generally advisable to use normal representatives in an experimental situation, but at the same time to be aware of the possibility that they may produce an exceptional effort, to reduce its impact so far as possible during the experiment, and to make such allowance as can be made for it when assessing results.

It is not only the representatives who may introduce bias into a test area during an experiment. Not infrequently a bias may be introduced by head-office management, at various levels, taking decisions affecting the experiment and being guided by what are normally quite sound marketing motives; but these may conflict with the needs of experimental discipline, the integrity of the test suffering as a result. This was the case in a projectable test launch carried out for a new product in one of the smaller television areas in Britain.

The product concerned was to be sold through food stores, and the company was already well known in the trade and had an established sales force calling on wholesalers and selected retailers. The general pattern of distribution of the new product was to be through wholesalers, with the major retailers being supplied directly. For the launch, the representatives would canvass additional retailers and pass their orders back through wholesalers for delivery and subsequent servicing.

The area was normally covered by three representatives, who were part of a team of seven under their area manager. At this level the representation in the area conformed to the general national level of the sales force as a whole. When the test launch was due to begin, the national sales manager found that he had two new recruits who had finished training but who had not been assigned to territories, and it would clearly do them no harm to take part in the test launch; they might gain some valuable experience from it. Consequently they were offered to the area manager concerned, who was glad to have them because the test operation was putting an additional load on his three men in the television area. These two were then also deployed in the area, making five representatives in all.

If the new product succeeded, as it was expected to, then sooner or later it would be put into the rest of the country under the charge of the remaining nine area managers. Clearly it would be useful if these nine could be given some first-hand experience in selling the new product, and arrangements were therefore made for them to move into the test area and to take part in the experiment. This raised the number of participants in the area to fourteen, apart from the local area manager, who was spending most of his time in this part of his area when he would normally have been spending only about half his time there.

Over and above this, the brand manager concerned, who had a very obvious interest in the test, went out to assess for himself the conditions and the problems in the field by taking a hand, followed by the regional supervisor, sales manager, and marketing director. All were acting from the best of motives, to see for themselves what was happening, to gain experience of the problems of selling this new product, and to gauge the reactions of the trade. The result of all this activity and interest, however, was that there were some eighteen or nineteen people operating in the area at various times and at various levels, as against the three and a half who would have been covering it under normal conditions.

In view of all this activity it was not altogether surprising that, at the end of three weeks, orders had been obtained from 80 per cent of the potential retail stockists of this product. Under normal conditions a distribution level of about 50 per cent would have been expected at the end of an eight-week cycle. In consequence, the product appeared on the market under test conditions so far removed from what could possibly happen if it was launched on a national basis that there was little hope of extracting from the results any valid estimate of the product's potential national performance.

This is an extreme, but well-documented and authentic, example of how a test can be wrecked and its objectives vitiated if no strict control is maintained over the whole operation and if management fails to take each successive decision against a background of experimental discipline. The motives for each decision were honourable, and there was no indication of their being taken with any conscious desire to sway the experiment's outcome. Most were taken in the belief that what was being done was for the ultimate benefit of the company in spreading experience in handling the new product. Nevertheless, because the active selling force was augmented to a level which could never be matched in any one area in a national launch, experimental discipline was violated and the operation was useless for assessing the likely national sales level.

Changing the variables

Other conflicts between the demands of experimental discipline and the natural inclinations of marketing men often arise when some aspect of an experiment fails to conform to expectation. This may happen when the distribution of a new product is sluggish, or when consumer awareness of a new product or campaign is slow to develop, or when purchasers do not appear, or when, having appeared, they take a long time to make repeat purchases. In any of these situations the true marketing man will quickly perceive ways in which he might apply some additional stimulus to bring progress back to his target levels – by augmenting his sales force, buying more time or space for advertising, changing his schedules, cutting his price, offering coupons, premiums, samples, money-back offers, and so on. In a small test area it may not be too difficult or too costly to organize any one of these methods quickly. Their use may well lead to improved levels of sales and possibly the achievement of the target levels in the test area. Furthermore, it is generally highly frustrating to the marketing man involved to believe, or even to know, that if he could only take some immediate action, then he would increase his chances of hitting the targets slipping beyond his reach.

But against the marketing man stands experimental discipline, insisting that any projected change in activities in the test area should be considered, not in the light of their effect in that area in the immediate future, but in the light of the basic objectives of the test and the feasibility of introducing identical modifications to the national marketing plan. In some cases, the situation certainly may allow a relaxation of experimental discipline and the introduction of a modification, either because the same modification can be introduced into any larger plan or because the objectives of the test can be modified to permit the change in plan.

Changing the objectives

For example, it may be legitimate to alter the marketing plan, even in a projectible test launch, when the marketing plan originally proposed has already been shown to have failed in producing at least some of the conditions necessary for the achievement of a profitable operation. In such a situation the original objectives have, in fact, already been achieved, the basic question answered and the plan proved a failure; but it may then be logical to stimulate this local market in some way which would not be available in a national launch so as to check on some specific aspects of, say, consumer purchasing behaviour, repeat buying, opinions about the product, its taste, texture, ease of use, etc., and to supplement the results of pretesting. Thus a product which has failed through inadequate distribution may be given some additional 'bought' outlets, so as to be able to test the extent of repurchase among those who have tried the product. While this may appear to be a relaxation of experimental discipline, it is more an adaptation of resources left over from one experiment to provide the basis for another of a more limited nature. Discipline must still, however, be maintained in any new experiment if bias is to be avoided. If the second experiment, for example, was aimed at assessing the rate of repurchase, the market could not be stimulated by price cutting since this might materially affect repurchase patterns and lead to biased results.

In opposite situations, where a test has produced disappointing but not completely negative results, and the basic questions the research was framed to answer remain open, nothing should be done in the area to stimulate results which could not subsequently form a part of a national marketing plan. Otherwise, if levels of performance are then achieved which are satisfactory, there will remain little chance of knowing whether these have been due to the new factors introduced, and which could never be repeated on a larger scale, or whether the original plan would have worked given time. Thus the results become biased, and the whole testing operation is rendered useless for the purposes for which it was designed.

There are some occasions in which modifications to the test plan can be made, because the changes can be accommodated in the national plan at a later stage. In general, to be fully effective the need for such changes must be recognized at a sufficiently early stage for appropriate action to be taken, and where there is delay it must be realized that the total effects of the modifications may not be fully reflected in the results obtained. Furthermore, since such modifications may well involve additional costs, their effects must be followed right through the marketing plan to a reassessment of profit levels and the sales levels necessary for the project being tested to become viable. In these circumstances even radical changes can sometimes be accommodated, as, for example, drafting in more representatives if the national plan can be revised to allow for successive area launches, when such local augmentation area by area across the country would be possible at a price.

Compromise

In practice, there must be some element of compromise between ideal experimental conditions and what is appropriate and possible from the marketing point of view. It is impossible to create in the market place the kind of conditions and rigid disciplines which can be achieved either in the laboratory or even in the course of agricultural field trials. In the laboratory all the conditions are under the control of the scientist, and he can regulate them at will. Furthermore he has the great advantage in most cases that, provided he does not choose conditions that damage his equipment, he can discontinue his experiment under one set of conditions and begin again with another set and the equipment will not remember that anything has changed. In the market place it is not possible to do this. If an experiment has been begun to test reactions to a price reduction and it does not produce the expected results, it is not generally possible to test another price in the same area with any hope of getting an unbiased result for some time.

The compromise in market experimentation is in ensuring that experimental discipline is observed so far as is possible, so as to avoid bias or any other deformation in the results. On the other hand, discipline must not be so rigidly enforced that the whole operation becomes artificial with the counterpart risk of the results becoming equally biased or misleading. For example, one aspect of experimental design which has not been mentioned, but on which the pure theoretician might insist, is that of randomization. The purist, offered a theoretical choice of fourteen television areas in which to test a new campaign or a new product, would insist on choosing the test areas at random, a process most easily, although not quite accurately, described as putting the names of all the areas into a hat and drawing out the required number for the test irrespective of any other factors relating to them. For most marketing experiments this may not be possible for reasons of cost, accessibility, manpower, known atypicality, or simply because an area is under the supervision of an area manager due to retire in twelve months and too inflexible to operate under the proposed conditions. Therefore the rigid application of experimental discipline in all its ramifications is hardly ever possible in marketing conditions.

While there is thus no room in experimental marketing for the rigid theorist who accepts only the full rigours of experimental philosophy and subjugates all aspects of the test to them, there is equally no place for those who abandon experimental discipline completely and who hold that, since it is not possible to control everything, there is no point in trying to control anything. While the former would probably lead to any test being abandoned as impracticable, the latter would lead to operations which would provide no safeguards against even the most elementary sources of bias and misleading results.

The simple, classical experimental situation is one in which all conditions are held equal except the one which is the object of the experiment. As experiments become more complex, they may be designed so as to allow more than one variable to change, as when chemical reactions are tested under conditions in which temperature and pressure are both varied. But however complicated the experiment may become, those conditions which are not designed to be varied in the plan are held to be constant. In marketing this can seldom be done, even in the most limited tests. In a small and limited test, for example, existing stocks of a product may be withdrawn from a single store and replaced with a new version in order to gain some preliminary estimate of the change's effect on sales. Conditions in the store may be fully controlled by giving the product its normal footage of shelf space in its normal position, and with all other competing products controlled in the same way. However, the extent to which control is possible is unlikely to include other stores in the neighbourhood, and any one of them may choose the period of the test to promote that particular product group, or one of the brands in it, by extra display, a price offer, or whatever. In consequence the sales in the test store may be affected – with or without the promoters of the test being aware of it – and the findings rendered of doubtful value.

In larger-scale operations in a wider environment, similar problems may arise from the normal activity within the market for the product; from natural or economic events outside the market but affecting it, such as abnormal weather, strikes in local industry or other such factors; or from the direct counter-activity of competitors. Some of these will affect the outcome of the experiment detrimentally, as when a product is one that reacts sharply to economic conditions and when the test area is subjected to a crippling strike in a major industry during the operation. In such a case no amount of experimental discipline will help, except through the point to be discussed later in Chapter 6 that tests should whenever possible be spread over more than a single area. It may be possible to make some adequate assessment of the outcome of the test, but certainly not under ideal conditions, since too many other factors will not have remained equal.

Competitive counter-activity

The problem of counter-activity by competitors raises questions which are by no means merely of academic interest since they have a direct bearing on the maintenance of experimental discipline and the test's integrity. In this context, counter-activity means activity by a competitor aimed specifically at the area in which the test is being mounted, although more general forms of activity on a wider scale which impinge on the test area as part of their effect may sometimes need similar consideration.

If the counter-activity is of a kind and on a scale which the competitor could be expected to mount nationally at a later stage, then in its way it will be contributing to the conditions which the project being tested will have to face in the wider market, and the test is being brought one stage nearer to real operational conditions. If, for example, during a pressure test in which the advertising appropriation in an area is raised by 50 per cent to assess whether it will yield additional profits a competitor increases his own activity in a way and to a level which he would be capable of doing in the wider market, then the test takes place under more realistic conditions than it would otherwise. The results will be even more valuable and revealing than if the competitor had stayed aloof. The same situation can arise on occasion in test launching, when two products from different manufacturers appear in the same test area, each obtaining as a result a far more realistic reading of his product's prospects than if it had been tested alone.

A more serious complication arises when a competitor in a test area takes action which he would find impossible on a national scale. This may take a number of forms, including increasing the advertising appropriation in the test area to a quite uneconomic level for the duration of the test; bringing in a local trade offer on generous terms so that efforts to sell the new product to the trade are frustrated because dealers' shelves are already loaded with that type of product; distributing coupons in the area, or distributing samples, so that the market is for a period distorted or depressed at the retail level; or even arranging for all supplies of a new product to be bought up as soon as they are delivered to the retailers. At present these and similar methods seem to be more common in other countries than in Britain, but some of them have been practised. The objective of the exercise, the type of product involved, and the nature of the change being tested all affect the extent to which these countermeasures can be invoked by competitors.

The decision on how to allow for any counter-activity brings us back to experimental discipline. If the activity is of a kind to be expected on the national market, like the normal wheeling and dealing operations associated with many consumer products, then this will presumably have been anticipated in formulating the national plan. Resources will have been set aside for use in such a situation, and it is then logical to take the appropriate action in the test area. This is not merely in line with experimental discipline; it is positively demanded by it. If, however, when faced with such normal counter-activity there is no contingent plan to meet it, then one must either be devised, and the consequent effects on all aspects of the project fully worked out with any necessary revisions of required levels of sales to achieve profitability, or else, if it is clear that no further resources can be committed, the experiment must be allowed to run its course to provide the requisite answers to the original questions posed. The alternative is to abandon it on the grounds that an effective answer has been obtained, i.e. that the project cannot proceed in the face of the competitive reaction which has been invoked and which would have to be met in any wider activity.

Looking at the question of counter-activity from the other side, there is frequently a good case for a manufacturer who is contemplating making such efforts against a competitor's experimental changes treating the counter-activity on a proper experimental basis. Thus if a competitor is experimenting with an increased appropriation, it may be far more useful to counter-attack at a level feasible on a national scale and to measure the results, than it would be merely to swamp the test area in an effort to stop the competitor learning anything from his own test. If a new product is being test launched, it may be better to use such counter-measures as price offers or coupons on a scale which could be repeated nationally, rather than to flood the area with samples on a vast scale in what may well prove a vain attempt to cause the product to be abandoned.

There is more to this than the detached scientific urge to measure and to learn, because the actions and reactions of competitors in a market clearly have long-term effects. In most cases, if one manufacturer is experimenting and another takes steps to wreck the experiment, it is unlikely that the project will be abandoned. The original experimenter may, in fact, find comfort in his project being regarded sufficiently seriously by his competitors for them to attempt to stop his progress towards national application. Wrecking a test will not necessarily stop the proposed national effort, and may even strengthen the resolve of those introducing it. On the other hand, if the innovation is met with counter-action in line with what would be possible on a wider scale, and this proves effective, the project is more likely to be abandoned. This may be particularly the case with marketing activities connected with existing products, when appropriate counter-activity may clearly demontrates that if one manufacturer introduces some such added effort as more advertising, lower price, more expensive packaging, etc., competitors will follow and the net result will merely be the continuance of existing unit sales levels and brand shares, but with increased costs and lower profits. Then the assessment of results would normally lead to the project being shelved and the status quo being maintained, whereas more violent retaliatory action would have prevented any valid assessment of the likely situation being made, and may merely have strengthened the originator's resolve to go ahead, on the assumption that his competitors are highly perturbed by his actions.

Sympathetic activity

Of less importance, but still requiring mention, is the problem of what may be called sympathetic activity, and this can make its appearance in various forms. It generally takes the form of special facilities provided by the owners of local media who have fostered experimental marketing activities in their areas, from which they may draw a not inconsiderable proportion of their revenue. These facilities may include, for example, special mailings to retailers in the areas to draw their attention to the proposed marketing activity, the organization of opportunities for the manufacturer to make contact with the trade, the provision of display material to link the product in the shops with the advertising, and so forth.

In many cases the provision of such facilities is of direct benefit to any manufacturer engaged in an experiment, since some such activity would be a part of his marketing plan and he would need to arrange for it to take place anyway. In other cases, however, there would be no intention or possibility of repeating these activities on a larger scale, and then the use of these facilities in the experimental areas would introduce un-wanted factors and run counter to experimental discipline. Since in many cases the whole package of time or space, the use of these facilities, and possibly even some of the research necessary to evaluate the results, is sold in one deal, those controlling the test must assess whether or not they should use the extra facilities as carefully as they would assess any other activities, and if necessary opt out of them in good time. Other-wise, the test may produce optimistic, misleading results in so far as the special facilities have an effect on either the trade or the consumers.

Measurement and interpretation

There is one final aspect of experimental discipline which needs to be mentioned, and that is the measurement and interpretation of results. There is clearly no point in carrying out an experiment unless the results are measured, and measured in such a way as to provide proper guidance in management decisions. Too often, well-planned and well-executed experiments fail to offer management all the information that could have been usefully obtained, because the measurements either were not of the right type, or were not made at the right points in the system, or were not made at the right times, or were not sufficiently accurate, or else because measurements inadequate to provide a proper basis for comparisons were made in areas outside the test.

The most common failing is that information is either not collected at the right points in the marketing system or else at not enough of them. The types of measurement which can be made, and their contributions to the interpretation of the results, will be covered more fully in Chapters 8 and 9, but there are some basic principles which need to be observed. In the first place, the ultimate assessment of the results will probably be made on the basis of changes in consumer sales, or the level of sales achieved by a new product. Thus some form of measurement of the flow of goods from the retailer to the consumer is required, and for many products this may be done in the store or the home. To provide a full picture even of the flow of goods, however, neither measurements made in the stores only nor measurements made on the consumer only will give the whole picture. The first will provide no data on the types of consumer buying the product or about the extent of repeat purchasing, while the second will provide no information about the extent of retail distribution or the adequacy of stocks. Thus, even to assess properly the flow of supplies, more than one set of measurements will be required.

In many experimental situations there is a second flow to be considered – the flow of information to the consumers, through advertising, display, and other means. This is seldom measured, and while the lack of such data may not be particularly serious if the sales of the product are well up to the levels sought, it is invaluable in assessing any operation where results have been lower than anticipated. If distribution has been achieved but consumers have not bought the product, data about the flow of information is essential if the weaknesses that have led to failure are to be identified. This should take the form of information on the numbers of potential consumers who had heard of the product by various times after the start of the experiment, their knowledge of it, their attitudes towards it, and so forth. Only from this is it possible to determine whether consumers remained unaware of the product, or whether they were made aware of it but not in a way which appealed to them, or if certain key points in the message were never registered, or if all the important information was put over without any effect; or if an effect was produced but prospective consumers were then put off by the packaging, the size, the shape, the price, or some other aspect.

It is very difficult to obtain this kind of information after the event, and so it must be collected during the course of the experiment if it is to have maximum value. Hence experimental discipline calls for a proper assessment during the planning stages of the types of information which will be needed to interpret the results, not only to decide whether or not the experiment as a whole is a success or failure, but also to assess the extent to which the various parts of the operation performed their allotted functions and contributed to the overall result.

In both test launching and in market testing – as when introducing a new campaign into certain areas, increasing the appropriation, using more representatives, changing the proportions of stores called on directly, or using coupons or other devices – data are also needed to record concurrent happenings in areas not subjected to the innovation so as to make proper comparisons. Thus arrangements must be made for the collection of the necessary control data, if it is not already available from existing research facilities.

For test launching there may sometimes be less of a need for comparative or 'control' data, but each case calls for individual consideration. In markets which are still developing, the introduction of a new brand frequently increases the rate of expansion, and full understanding of the test results can only be achieved if the extent of the expansion can be assessed by comparing test area results with data on the performance of the product group in other areas. In more fully developed markets, where the new product offers no radical advance on those already available, it may sometimes be possible to work without control data, but as soon as any major product advance that may lead to expansion of the market is involved, control data is again needed for full interpretation of the results.

Implementation

While much of this chapter may sound discouraging to those engaged in marketing, it is not too difficult to plan and implement proper marketing experiments. Any experiment must take a certain amount of time, money, and other resources to organize, and generally the additional efforts required to ensure that it is properly organized are not prohibitive. The difference in the results can be of paramount importance, since biased or otherwise misleading results may lead to decisions being wrongly taken and to a consequent loss of considerable sums of money.

A badly designed or ill-controlled test may not infrequently be worse than no test at all, partly because it is not always easy to detect misleading results, and also because there is sometimes a possibility that harassed executives will accept its results without making a full critical appraisal. While, without a test, something approaching the right answer may be achievable, the results of poorly designed or inadequate experiments will at best cause confusion and at worst may lead to uneconomic decisions.

Thus the choice is often not so much between one version of a test as being better than another, as deciding whether if one cannot have the best version one should even attempt to use an alternative. The answer will inevitably depend on the nature of the test and the decisions which rest on it. If critical decisions on whether or not to enter a market, or on the amount of capital to invest in plant, etc., depend on the outcome of a projectable test launch, then the whole operation must be carried out as scientifically as marketing conditions allow and with a full range of measurements from which to make the final assessments. On the other hand, if a small test is being carried out with, say, a wire dispenser in a limited number of shops, merely to assess whether it remains stable and functions properly under real use conditions, there are few problems in organizing an appropriate experiment. Shops may well be selected for such a test because they are atypical – those, for instance, with a high turnover of the product or with crowded aisles – where selective use of such shops to measure a test launch would be misleading.

Experimental discipline must be observed if valid results are to be obtained from any test, but the extent to which this will make demands on the organization or impose limitations will depend on the nature of the test and the use to which the results are to be put. There can be little doubt that marketing experiments must be controlled by marketing personnel, since they are the experts in the techniques being tested and since they know, or should know, the environment in which the test is taking place. They will, however, be involved in the test to a greater or lesser extent and will generally lack a background of experimental discipline; even if one person or team can combine marketing knowledge and experimental discipline, it can still remain difficult to allow the latter its proper scope in the face of a marketing crisis. For these reasons it is advisable in most cases, and particularly with more important experiments, to introduce into the team concerned with the experiment someone from outside with a background of experimental discipline, giving him a brief to watch the whole situation and to make proper representations if the integrity of the test is likely to be impaired.

When a clash occurs between the needs of the marketing situation and the needs of experimental discipline, then some rational decision must be reached in the light of the circumstances. It may be in some cases that the marketing situation itself precludes the establishment and operation of any valid test, and once this becomes clear then decisions must be reached without the benefit of experimental results. In other cases, a compromise may be reached between the marketing situation and the application of rigid experimental discipline permitting the test to continue but with some possible reservations about those aspects of the results which may be affected. In still other cases, experimental discipline must prevail if the results are to have any real meaning within the context of the original problem.

The demands of experimental discipline may at times make life difficult, and in any field of experimentation, even in the physical sciences, it can often prove hard to produce satisfactory experimental results that are free from bias or ambiguity. In marketing it may be just that much more difficult, because of the large number of factors involved in each situation, not all of which can be controlled. The proper use of experimental discipline will ensure that the results obtained are valid attempts to answer the questions originally posed, and that as such they can be accepted as a basis for subsequent discussions and decisions. Without the acceptance of discipline, results will still be obtained in the form of percentages, ratios, quantities, market shares, etc., but if they are obtained under the wrong conditions, they may well be biased and misleading and carry the unavoidable risk of wrong decisions being taken that will cost far more in the long run than more careful or rigorous experimentation would have done.

3

When to use projectable test launching

Many of the projectable test launches at present being undertaken are unprofitable in that they are worth less than the costs of carrying them out. This situation arises partly because the costs of testing are frequently underestimated through certain items being left out of the reckoning; partly because failure to use available data to its full potential often creates an impression that more research is needed before a decision can be reached; partly because the objectives and the criteria for assessment are not defined in advance; and partly because decisions are too often taken only within the framework of the three options of *launch*, *test*, or *abandon*, other potentially profitable options being ignored. Sometimes, alas, it is only too apparent that testing has been chosen as a soft option and as a means of deferring the critical choice between *launch* or *abandon* for six or twelve months.

There is no simple formula to solve the problem of whether or not to test, but there are methods of approaching it which will lead towards easier and better decisions, and these form the basis of this chapter.

Prerequisite conditions

There are, of course, certain conditions which must be met before any form of testing can be considered at all, including the facilities for providing supplies of the product in the quantities likely to be required for the test on an economic basis. In some cases this may be possible through imports, with some necessary modification, repackaging or re-labelling to conform to the specifications of the planned product and marketing mix. In other cases it may not be difficult or unduly expensive to set up the limited production facilities needed for the test, or else supplies may be available from a pilot plant. With some products, however, the establishment of actual production facilities may call for a virtually full investment in plant capable of producing on a national scale, the decision to test thus pre-empting the decision that the testing is supposed to clarify and so making it largely pointless or hopelessly uneconomic.

Competitive factors

Less tangible but equally real problems arise concerning the competitive advisability of testing. Testing in the open market obviously involves disclosure of the new product or innovation itself, but it also means that any competitor prepared to observe and measure the results for himself can form his own assessments of the likely market potential indicated by the test. The risks involved in such disclosure will usually depend on four main factors:

1 The time it would take for competitors to develop a similar or better product on the basis of their existing knowledge.
2 The nature of the competitors themselves.
3 The resources available to them.
4 The market potential involved.

If the new product is the result of research which is far ahead of the rest of the industry, perhaps using new processes or methods adequately protected by patents or other safeguards, the problem of disclosure may be minimized. Competitors cannot follow, although they may take other action to strengthen their existing positions before any national launch. If, however, the innovation can be quickly introduced by a competitor, factors 2, 3 and 4 need to be considered. Aggressive competition, backed by adequate resources to take risks and combined with a large potential market, could rule out any test operation because of the likelihood of competitive pre-emption in the wider market. With less aggressive competition, competition hampered by lack of ready resources or with only a small market potential at stake, testing may involve no great risks of pre-emption.

There is a developing field of study known as 'Game Theory' which is concerned with problems of this type, where there are a number of 'players' or competitors, each with certain resources and each with a series of options open to him, while rewards and penalties are distributed according to the ways in which the various options are exercised. By assessing or assigning probabilities to the ways in which competitors are likely to exercise their options in the face of such specific actions as test launching by one of them, numerical values can be placed on the risks, penalties and rewards of testing or immediate launching. So far, however, the theory is not capable of dealing with highly complex situations, and for practical purposes this is not yet a useful means of reaching decisions in this area. It is thus outside the scope of this book, but those with a mathematical bent may find it an interesting field for further study.

Risk factors

Once the broad problems of the availability of the product and the competitive advisability of testing have been resolved, there remain two other sets of linked considerations. These are the 'risk' factors, involving first the magnitude of the profits or losses which would result under varying conditions of planning and achievement; and secondly the probability of any one particular set of conditions arising and so leading to a particular profit or loss.

For a full appreciation of the risks, both these factors of magnitude and probability must be recognized, but since the likely range of results is easier to assess than the probabilities, this is the aspect considered first.

When considering the introduction of a new product it is customary to assess the levels of profit or loss which would result if various hypothetical quantities were produced and sold. The range of quantities which these calculations cover may be quite narrow if, on the basis of knowledge and experience, the company can already make a fairly precise forecast of the likely level of sales, though in other cases the range may be quite wide. These calculations are valuable for showing how much variation there is from one end of the range to the other, whether all levels will show profits, or whether there will be losses at the lower end of the scale. These data alone, however, are not enough to offer grounds for a full appreciation.

Planning levels and levels of achievement

The next step is to produce a series of calculations of a similar nature, but on the basis of planning being on an expectation of one level, and achievement being eventually on another.

For example, if plans are based on an expected level of sales of 300 cases a year, what would be the profit or loss if the sales levels achieved were only 200 cases, or reached 400 cases?* The figures obtained will generally be different from those obtained on the basis of both planning and achievement being on the basis of 200 or 400 cases, since such factors as fixed overheads on unused plant capacity will make the 200 level less profitable than if it had been planned for, while pushing production to 400 on plant designed for 300 may lead to increased costs

* Small amounts are used here for typographical convenience.

through overtime or increased waste or other factors. The results will differ from one product to another, depending on the extent to which production depends on heavy investment that cannot be quickly changed, or whether there have been other heavy setting-up costs in training or other ways.

The profit-and-loss matrix

Given these results at suitable intervals over the likely range of sales levels, any pattern which they contain is best seen by arranging them in a table or matrix, as in Figure 3.1. Here the rows are labelled with the possible planning levels of production and sales, and the columns are labelled with the possible levels of achievement when the product is marketed. At this stage no attention is paid to the probabilities of any particular outcome happening, but merely to the estimated sums of profit and loss which could occur on the basis of the pairings of planned and achieved levels.

Figure 3.1 Matrix of profits and losses: example 1

Levels of achievement (cases)

Expected or planning levels (cases), £/$:

	100	150	200	250	300	350	400	450
100	0	0	0	0	0	0	0	0
150	0	0	0	0	0	0	0	0
200	−400	−200	0	50	100	150	200	250
250	−500	−300	−100	100	150	200	250	300
300	−600	−400	−200	0	200	250	300	350
350	−700	−500	−300	−100	100	300	350	400
400	−800	−600	−400	−200	0	200	400	450
450	−900	−700	−500	−300	−100	100	300	500

Individual companies may work on different bases for assessing costs before arriving at the values to be put into the table. Some, for example, may work simply on costs and revenue, so that all 'profit' is contained in the figures calculated. Others may demand that a minimum level of profit, calculated perhaps as a return on capital or as a percentage on turnover, is regarded as a cost and must be covered by a new product before it can be considered viable. However, the precise form of the calculations does not matter in the discussion which follows, always provided that whatever form is used is applied consistently through all the calculations.

There are problems of time involved here in two senses. First there is the unit of time over which results are to be assessed; in the simplest situations this may be taken as a year, but it can be either the first year of operation or a 'normal' year after the product has settled in the market. There is no reason, however, why the calculations described should not be based on longer periods, or why more sophisticated figures based, for instance, on discounted cash flows or present worth should not be used in place of the simple profit-and-loss figures.

The second time problem concerns the speed with which modifications can be made to plans should the achieved rate not equal the planned rate. A manufacturer who has planned on the basis of producing and selling 500 cases of a product a year and who is faced with demand for only 300 will adjust his plans to the new figures as quickly as possible, but there will be some delays and some factors which may not be amenable to adjustment, such as plant of excessive capacity. Similarly, if demand exceeds the planned levels it may take time to adjust to the new levels as well as incurring extra costs while the adjustments are being made.

Some compromises may need to be accepted before the values to appear in the table resulting from any mis-matching of plans and achievements are arrived at, but this should not stop the calculations being made. In so far as novel problems are presented here, this is only because the method brings them to light where less extensive calculations would leave them concealed.

The figures in Figure 3.1 are hypothetical, but are based on the idea of a product carrying high initial or capital costs and heavy penalties for over- or under-estimating the market. A later example will show somewhat different conditions and patterns.

The break-even point

The first point to note in Figure 3.1 is that there is a 'break-even point', showing neither profit nor loss, when plans and achievement match at 200 cases, giving zero profit. It is a necessary condition of a break-even point that the planned and achieved levels associated with it match and these points should not be confused with other points in the table where zeros occur but planning and achievement do not match – as, for example, if plans were made for 300 cases, but sales of only 250 cases were achieved. There is normally only one break-even point in a table of this type, but in some situations, where plant has to be installed in large units and costs thus follow a step-function, there may be two or more. This does not affect the issue, beyond complicating it.

The row and column in which the break-even point falls divide the matrix naturally into four parts. In the upper left quadrant the rows denote planned or 'expected' levels of sales of less than the break-even level, and thus losses would be expected should the product be launched. At the same time, the values at the tops of the columns indicate that similar low levels of achievement which would lead to losses would, in fact, be experienced in a launch. Thus in this quadrant the expected outcome is too poor for the product to be launched and this decision would be right. All values here are zero.

The upper right quadrant covers the area in which expectation is still below the break-even level, so that the product would not logically be marketed, but where this expectation would be proved wrong because a viable level of sales could, in fact, be achieved. Since, however, the logical decision would be to abandon the product, or at least refer it back for further development, no surplus will be earned in any cell in this quadrant and again all values are zero.

In the lower left quadrant, the expected levels of sales are greater than the break-even level, but the actual outcome would be sales at less than the break-even level and all values in this quadrant are negative. They will be the losses incurred by planning on the expectation of various profitable levels of operation, and then being faced with one of a range of levels of failure.

The lower right quadrant contains all the profitable combinations of expectations and achievement, but it may also contain some negative values or losses. This is normally the only area in which traditional calculations are made, and even then they tend to be made only for selected values on the diagonal where plans and achievement are equated. It should be noted that losses can still be recorded in this quadrant even though all achievements are above the break-even level, through the planning level being far above the achieved level and so leading to an uneconomic operation.

The values in the matrix are calculated on the basis of the set of such marketing parameters as price, advertising appropriation, sales force, promotional expenditure, etc., which it is proposed to use in the wider launch. Sometimes, however, not all these sums have been settled when test launching is being considered, and it is then possible to build up a series of matrices to cover the main sets of alternative values. These will then indicate the shapes of the problems at various levels and may show that some combinations lead to wider variations in the profits and losses, and thus to situations which are inherently more risky than others.

Profit-and-loss contours

A matrix of the type shown in Figure 3.1 provides a basis for gaining considerable insight into a market situation. It will be seen that the levels of profit and loss do not change evenly over the surface, but that the rate of change is greater in some parts than in others. In Figure 3.2 contour lines linking points with equal profit or loss have been drawn over the original figures, and the different slopes in different parts of the matrix are clearly visible. To the right of the matching diagonal the contours run in a 'north-easterly' direction, and are widely spaced,

Figure 3.2 Matrix of profits and losses: example 1

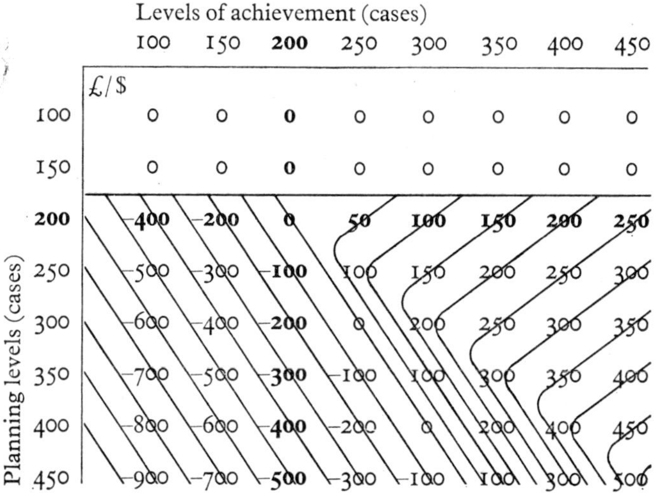

indicating a moderate degree of elasticity in profits as volume changes. Any level of achievement greater than the planned levels will increase profits, but on a moderate basis. For example, on a planned basis of 350 cases which would yield 300 units of profit if achieved, an increase in achievement to 400 cases, a rise of 14 per cent, would provide fifty extra units of profits, or an increase of 16 per cent. This, however, is only half of the additional profit obtainable if planning had originally been at the 400-case level.

To the left of the matching diagonal the contour lines in Figure 3.2

behave quite differently, running in a 'north-west south-east' direction and being much closer together. In this case the contours show that failure to reach the planned level, whatever that may be, will have an immediate and serious effect on the outcome. Failure to achieve the planned level of 350 units by only fifty units, a drop of 14 per cent, leads to a fall in the profit from 300 units to 100, a fall of 67 per cent, compared with 200 units of profit at the correct planning level.

The fact that the elasticity of the surplus is different, as often happens, on the two sides of the matching diagonal (or, in certain circumstances, possibly between other sub-areas of the matrix) has obvious implications in the processes of deciding the level of activity to be planned for, and this will be discussed later.

The relative loss matrix

The maximum profits for each level of achievement are earned when planning has been correctly based on attaining that level. These are the values along the matching diagonal. Whenever planning is on a basis not matched by achievement, a lower level of return is obtained, the difference being the penalty for not correctly matching demand. The penalties or relative losses (i.e. relative to what might have been made) can be obtained by subtracting each value in Figure 3.1 from the value on the matching diagonal in the same column, and these figures can be entered in a similar relative loss matrix, as in Figure 3.3.

Figure 3.3 Matrix of relative losses: example 1

Levels of achievement (cases)

Planning levels (cases)	£/$ 100	150	**200**	250	300	350	400	450
100	0	0	**0**	−100	−200	−300	−400	−500
150	0	0	**0**	−100	−200	−300	−400	−500
200	−400	−200	**0**	−50	−100	−150	−200	−250
250	−500	−300	**−100**	0	−50	−100	−150	−200
300	−600	−400	**−200**	−100	0	−50	−100	−150
350	−700	−500	**−300**	−200	−100	0	−50	−100
400	−800	−600	**−400**	−300	−200	−100	0	−50
450	−900	−700	**−500**	−400	−300	−200	−100	0

This matrix differs from the previous one in that it now has values in the top right quadrant, and that all figures are negative or zero. The zeros occupy the positions where the appropriate level of achievement was planned for, and thus there is no penalty or relative loss for being wrong – along the matching diagonal and in the top left quadrant where the overall decision not to market at planning levels below break-even 'matches' any level of achievement less than break-even.

The values in the top right quadrant now represent the losses suffered by the company in not launching a product which would have achieved some level of demand above the break-even level, and all rows are the same, representing the optimum profit obtainable at each level of achievement.

It is now seen that the minimum penalty for overestimating the market by fifty cases is 100 units of profit, while the minimum penalty for underestimation is fifty units of profit. These figures now begin to fix the boundaries within which a projectable test launch can be beneficial, for it must be able to specify the level of achievement which will be reached in the major market for less than the cost of finding out in the major market itself. In general, the smaller the levels of relative losses shown in the matrix, the less need there is for testing, since use of the wrong planning level will not prove to be very expensive and may well be less than the cost of testing. Where, however, as in Figure 3.3, any movement away from the matching diagonal leads to large relative losses which may far exceed the costs of testing, there is a much stronger case for a projectable test launch.

Another product

Before proceeding to discuss this further, examples of the possible matrices for a product not involving heavy initial investment and where the planned volume can be rapidly adjusted to achievement are shown in Figures 3.4 and 3.5. These matrices are constructed in the same way as before, but it will be noticed that the gradients in Figure 3.4 are much more gentle and that the relative losses in Figure 3.5 are only of a minor nature. For example, if achievement is 450 cases, a planned level as low as 300 cases will still return profits of 120 units and a planned level of 550 cases a profit of 130 units compared with the optimum level of 150 units. The penalties are therefore only of the order of −20 or −14 per cent for failing to plan to the achieved sales level by −33 or +22 per cent.

Figure 3.4 Matrix of profits and losses: example 2

Levels of achievement (cases)

£/$	200	250	**300**	350	400	450	500	550
200	O	O	**0**	O	O	O	O	O
250	O	O	**0**	O	O	O	O	O
300	−120	−60	**0**	40	80	**120**	160	200
350	−130	−70	**−10**	50	90	130	170	210
400	−140	−80	**−20**	40	100	140	180	220
450	−150	−90	**−30**	30	90	150	190	230
500	−160	−100	**−40**	20	80	140	200	240
550	−170	−110	**−50**	10	70	130	190	250

Planning levels (cases)

Figure 3.5 Matrix of relative losses: example 2

Levels of achievement (cases)

£/$	200	250	**300**	350	400	450	500	550
200	O	O	**0**	−50	−100	−150	−200	−250
250	O	O	**0**	−50	−100	−150	−200	−250
300	**−120**	**−60**	**0**	**−10**	**−20**	**−30**	**−40**	**−50**
350	−130	−70	**−10**	0	−10	−20	−30	−40
400	−140	−80	**−20**	−10	0	−10	−20	−30
450	−150	−90	**−30**	−20	−10	0	−10	−20
500	−160	−100	**−40**	−30	−20	−10	0	−10
550	−170	−110	**−50**	−40	−30	−20	−10	0

Planning levels (cases)

Probabilities

The figures in the matrices are, however, only estimates of the outcome to be expected when plans laid on one basis of sales are met by achievement at some yet unknown level. To interpret and use the data fully, and even to determine the position and size of the matrix, it is necessary to consider the degree of certainty or uncertainty surrounding these possible levels of achievement.

Before a product is anywhere near test launching, management will have developed some idea of the likely range of sales to be expected that will limit the total range of values between zero and infinity which might otherwise have to be considered. There may well be a number of forecasts based on assumptions of different levels of initial promotion, prices, or other marketing factors, and if the company still has its options open to launch using different marketing plans, separate matrices can be constructed for each plan.

The reliability of the forecasts at this stage will depend on such factors as the amount of data available about the market, the data available about the new product from laboratory or consumer testing, the experience of the personnel involved, and so forth. The forecasts themselves may be expressed in a number of ways, some of which will reflect the degree of uncertainty, e.g. a forecast that sales will probably lie in the range of 400 to 550 units; or will be about 1,000 units $\pm$200 units. Where there is a great deal of uncertainty about the forecast, the range will be wide, but where there is considerable experience with similar products in the past, backed by research data on the current one, the range may be comparatively narrow.

The matrix developed for a new product should cover the full range of sales levels which are 'likely' to be achieved, but should not be unnecessarily extended to cover levels which, while technically possible, are most 'unlikely' to arise. Thus the question of the probability with which various levels of achievement might be realized becomes a prime factor in determining the range and content of the matrix itself, and terms more precise than 'likely' and 'unlikely' are necessary.

If, instead of attempting to forecast the sales levels of a new product, the problem was to forecast the numbers of times an unbiased coin would fall heads up in one hundred tosses, the problem would be simple. Calculation, or reference to appropriate tables, would show that the probability of getting fewer than thirty-eight heads is ·01, and a table could be drawn up showing the probabilities of the number falling in each of the possible ranges as follows.

Number of heads	Probability of occurrence
—32	·00
33–37	·01
38–42	·06
43–47	·24
48–52	·38
53–57	·24
58–62	·06
63–67	·01
68+	·00

Given this data, it is possible to assess the precise effect of taking any particular boundary between the 'likely' and the 'unlikely'. The range of values between forty-three and fifty-seven heads, for example, contains levels of achievement with a combined probability of occurrence which adds up to ·86, or which would cover the achieved result on 86 per cent of occasions. Generally in statistical work there is a tradition – it is no more than that – that it is adequate to cover the 95 per cent level of expectation, and on that basis it would be sufficient in working on the 'heads' data to concentrate on the range from about forty heads to about sixty. The chance of other results occurring is sufficiently unlikely to justify leaving them out of account.

In a marketing situation precise levels of probability cannot be calculated in this way. The probabilities put against any possible level of achievement will be subjective, based perhaps in part on numerical results from research, but also to some extent at least on experience. It is therefore unrealistic to expect 95 per cent limits to be set as precisely as they can be for experiments into tossing coins, but the same objective is being pursued, however imprecise may be the means of reaching it. Further, the various levels within the matrix need to be assigned probabilities before they can be used to their full potential for deciding whether or not test launching is justified.

Since people do not generally think in terms of probabilities – we may think it looks like rain, but we seldom if ever think there is an 80 per cent chance of it raining – it is necessary to devise some simple method for transforming normal thoughts of likelihood into some numerical measures of probability. One of the simplest methods is to give the most likely event in the range being considered ten points or marks, and then to give each alternative an appropriate number based on an assessment of the relative probability of it happening. Thus ten marks are allotted to the level of sales considered most likely, and then the next most likely level is considered. If it is thought to be only slightly less probable than the first one, it may be given a mark of eight or nine; if it is only thought to be about half as likely, a mark of five is given, and so forth. The process is continued until there are no further values which would deserve a mark of one or more. The total number of marks allocated is now summed, and each individual mark is expressed as a proportion or percentage of the total. The result is a series of probabilities which can be used to determine the limits of the matrix and in interpreting the results.

If the range of values covered in this operation is wide, then it is likely that the probabilities or percentages attached to some of the less likely values will be small, and it may be possible to limit the range of the matrix by taking only the levels covered by the central 90 or 95 per cent of probabilities.

This procedure may be extended from a situation where a single individual is making the assessments to a committee situation. The same procedure would be followed for each member of the committee or management concerned with making the estimates, each set of marks percentaged within itself and an average taken of the various sets. If all concerned are considered to have equal aptitude in making forecasts, or equal authority, or equal responsibility, or whatever criterion may be useful, then a simple average will give equal weight to each set of opinions. There is no reason, however, why the assessments made by the more able or experienced should not be weighted by multiplying them by some factor before adding them into the calculations, the sums being divided by the totals of the weights used to give the final set of probabilities.

The matrix with probabilities

The set of probabilities used in the calculations which follow should add to unity, or to 100 per cent if they are being expressed in percentages. If the range has been truncated by leaving off some of the minor values, the situation is best restored to the required state by adding the probabilities of the truncated values in to the probabilities of the remaining values nearest to them. The final probabilities are then entered into the matrix in the columns to which they refer, and no other columns need be considered further.

Before undertaking the work of calculating the levels of profit and loss for all the positions in the matrix, the break-even point should be established, and its position in relation to the new matrix considered. If the break-even quantity is lower than any of the values now contained in the matrix, this means that the whole of the operative part of the matrix lies in the lower right quadrant, that all levels of achievement are potentially profitable if they are properly forecast, and that all points in the matrix should be calculated. If the break-even level is higher than any level contained in the matrix, no level of achievement foreseen will be profitable and the operation should not proceed to market on a test or any other basis. If the break-even falls within the range of the matrix, the situation is as shown in the previous diagrams, and calculations should be made for the points in the two lower quadrants. For illustration, part of the matrix shown in Figure 3.1 is reproduced here as Figure 3.6, but now with a set of probabilities shown across the columns. The values omitted are those whose achievement is deemed to have only negligible probabilities of occurring.

Figure 3.6 Matrix with probabilities

| | Levels of achievement (cases) | | | | | |
	150	200	250	300	350	400
£/$						
200	−200	0	50	100	150	200
250	−300	−100	100	150	200	250
300	−400	−200	0	200	250	300
350	−500	−300	−100	100	300	350
400	−600	−400	−200	0	200	400
P=	·10	·25	·30	·20	·10	·05

(Row labels under "Planning levels (cases)")

The first point to look for is whether there are any losses on the left-hand side of the matrix. If none appear, it will be possible to proceed to operate at any of the levels included in the matrix in the knowledge that, if the assessed probabilities are well-founded, there is no risk of an absolute loss on the launch. The problem remains, however, of establishing the optimum level at which to plan, and this may call for a test launch.

When losses appear in the matrix, as in Figure 3.6, the first question is whether the company could accept such losses without being crippled or wound up – or possibly even whether the executives responsible for the project could accept such losses without similar effects on their careers. At this stage, this is not a question of risk, or whether the acceptance of the risk of such losses is justified by the expectation of profits, but merely whether the company will be able to stand such a loss at all if it arises. If the company, or the executives, could not survive a level of loss in the matrix, then the planning level associated with it should not be used without further information. If all rows contain such losses, the company then has only two options open: either to undertake further research, such as a test launch, or to abandon the project.

Where a matrix contains some rows which are acceptable (i.e. wholly profitable or only containing acceptable losses) and some which cannot be accepted because of the sizes of the losses, the company has an option either to launch immediately within the acceptable range at the level expected to yield maximum profit on the available data or to test to acquire more data.

Study of the matrix to this stage should leave the company with one of two pairs of options: either to test or to launch immediately; or, to test or abandon. In either case the next stage of calculation is involved.

Expectations before testing

The data now consists of the profits and losses shown in the operative part of the matrix and the assessments of the probabilities that each of a range of levels of achievement will be reached. These can now be combined to show the 'expectations' in profit or loss of acting on each of the planning levels on the basis of existing knowledge.

The expectation can be described as the likely average result if the product was to be launched many times, and the assessed probabilities applied. Taking the planning level of 200 cases as an example, over many trials, and converting the probabilities to percentages for ease of description, then a loss of 200 units of profit would be expected to occur on 10 per cent of the trials. Similarly, a zero profit would be expected in 25 per cent of trials, a profit of fifty units in 30 per cent of trials and so forth. Thus the average result over a series of trials, or the average expectation from a single trial, would be the sum of the products of the probabilities and the results to which they refer. For the row denoting planning at the 200-case level, in Figure 3.6, this would be:

$$-200 \times \cdot 1 + 0 \times \cdot 25 + 50 \times \cdot 3 + 100 \times \cdot 2$$
$$+ 150 \times \cdot 1 + 200 \times \cdot 05 = +40 \text{ units of profit}$$

The expectations from planning on the remaining levels on the basis of present information can be calculated in the same way to give the following table of results.

Figure 3.7 Expectations without testing

		Levels of achievement (cases)							Expectation of profit
		150	200	250	300	350	400		
	£/$								
Planning levels (cases)	200	−20	0	15	20	15	10	→	40
	250	−30	−25	30	30	20	12·5	→	37·5
	300	−40	−50	0	40	25	15	→	−10
	350	−50	−75	−30	20	30	17·5	→	−87·5
	400	−60	−100	−60	0	20	20	→	−180
P =		·10	·25	·30	·20	·10	·05		

The right-hand column of the table shows the present expectation of profit at each planning level calculated on the basis of the existing information and the assessment of the probabilities of achieving the various levels of sales.

From these results it is seen that it would be possible to plan immediately on a basis of either 200 cases or 250 cases in the expectation of profits of 40 units and 37½ units respectively. Launching at any higher level on present information would lead to expectations of losses, and these levels cannot therefore rationally be used at this stage as a basis for planning a profitable venture.

Of the two potentially profitable levels, 200 cases shows a higher expectation of profit than the 250 level, even though the ascribed probabilities give the 250 level a higher probability of being realized in itself. This is because the balance of probabilities and rewards differs between the rows.

At this stage the company could, if it were so inclined, proceed to market immediately in the expectation of profits on a modest basis and provided it could accept the absolute loss of 200 or 300 units of profit if the one in ten chance of achieving only 150 cases of sales can be accepted.

If, as could well happen with a different set of figures in the matrix, or with a different set of probabilities, all the levels of planning gave expectations of losses, then on a coldly logical basis immediate marketing is ruled out at any viable level.

If all rows show expectations of profit, the company can proceed to market at the level giving the greatest expectation of profit, provided it can accept any risk of absolute loss indicated in the previous figures (in Figure 3.6). However, this may not be the true optimum level, and it will be worth completing the calculations of the effect of introducing a test launch to assess the likely gains through doing so.

Probabilities generated by testing

The next problem is therefore the extent to which a projectable test launch would add to the information already available, i.e. how far would it modify the range of probabilities in the matrix and the expectations of profits.

No test operation will be completely accurate, and the reliability of such an exercise will depend on a number of factors, including the nature of the product, the pattern of consumer purchases, the types of outlet and so forth, and this problem is discussed further in Chapter 9. For purposes of illustration, we will assume here that there is a 60 per cent chance that the results will be accurate within the size categories used in the matrix, a 30 per cent chance that the readings overestimate the true position by one category, and a 10 per cent chance that they underestimate by one category. This is not an unreasonable set of assumptions.

This would mean that if a projectable test launch led to a forecast of sales of 250 cases, it would indicate a 30 per cent chance of achieving 200 cases, a 60 per cent chance of achieving 250 cases, and a 10 per cent chance of achieving 300 cases. Thus we can now draw up another matrix to show the probabilities of achieving the various levels of sales if the various possible levels of test results are obtained (Figure 3.8). For the purist, there is a slight anomaly in putting the figure of ·6 into the lower right-hand corner, but this is not likely to affect the result.

Figure 3.8 Probabilities generated by testing

| | Levels of achievement (cases) | | | | | |
	150	200	250	300	350	400
Test forecast (cases) 200	·3	·6	·1			
250		·3	·6	·1		
300			·3	·6	·1	
350				·3	·6	·1
400					·3	·6

Expectations with testing

The final stage is to combine this set of probabilities which could arise from testing with the expectations in Figure 3.7, and so get expectations based on all currently available data. It is done by multiplying each figure in Figure 3.7 by the corresponding probability in Figure 3.8 and summing across the rows. The effect of this is to bring into one figure the probability of a particular test result occurring, the assessed probability of reaching a particular level of achievement, and the profit or loss if planning proceeds on the basis of the test result. This then shows the 'contribution' to the total expectation of profits made by each cell in the matrix.

Since a level of 200 cases has already been established as the break-even level, there is no point in carrying out calculations for any test result below this level as no launch would be carried out. Figure 3.9 shows the results, with the rows added across. They indicate that

Figure 3.9 Calculation of expectation with testing

Test forecast (cases)	Levels of achievement (cases)						Sums of rows
	150	200	250	300	350	400	
200	−6	0	1·5				−4·5
250		−7·5	18	3			13·5
300			0	24	2·5		26·5
350				6	18	1·75	25·75
400					6	12	18

Expectation of profit 83·75

should a test forecast of 200 cases be obtained, the contribution to the expectation would now be a loss and so no launch could be planned at this level. The outcome would therefore be no action, and no profit or loss. The remaining rows, denoting test results ranging from 250 to 400 cases, show a combined expectation of profit at this stage of 83·75 units. This is the assessment of the expectation of profits which would result after testing, using the test data to reach decisions on the optimum level of operation. The figure should now be compared with the best expectation of profits if the product was launched without testing. In Figure 3.7 this would have been 40 units of profit from launching immediately at a planned level of 200 cases. The decision of whether to test or not would now basically depend on whether or not the costs of testing exceeded 44 units of profit, which is the gain in expectation obtained through testing.

It may appear anomalous that if the product was to be launched immediately without testing, the planning level of 200 cases gives the highest expectation of profits, whereas, if testing is undertaken, the lowest test estimate offering any expectation of profits is 250 cases. The reason, of course, is that with present pre-test knowledge alone it is believed that there is a 65 per cent chance of sales exceeding the 200-unit level. A test result itself indicating sales of 200 cases would destroy this hope, since it would give only a 10 per cent chance of sales of 250 cases and no chance of any higher level. A low test result would so modify the probabilities of achieving the various levels, that what previously appeared to be a profitable operation comes to be seen as hazardous, the belief that there were good chances of reaching some of the higher levels of sales having been shattered.

It is useful to work out the expectations of profit which can be expected after testing, on the assumption that each level in turn has been forecast by the test and is now the basis for planning. If the 200-case level was predicted by the test, then, using the assumptions about the accuracy of the test given above, and the profits and losses from Figure 3.6, there would be a 30 per cent chance of achieving 150 cases, giving a loss of 200 units of profit; a 60 per cent chance of achieving 200 cases of sales at a break-even level of zero profit; and a 10 per cent chance of achieving 250 cases generating 50 units of profit. The expectation of profits given a test result of 200 cases, transformed into a planning level of 200 cases, is obtained as before:

$$-200 \times \cdot 3 + 0 \times \cdot 6 + 50 \times \cdot 1 = -55$$

The same calculation is applied to each of the other planning levels, matching the planning level to the indicated result of the test in each case to give the following table:

Test forecast cases	Expectation of profit if launch planned on test forecast
200	−55
250	45
300	145
350	245
400	340

The expectation for a test result of 150 is not included, since the product would not be launched at that level, which is below the break-even point, and the row has already been discarded from the matrix. In calculating the expectation at the 400 level, where the probability of reaching 450 cases has already been ruled out as having zero probability, it has been assumed that only two probabilities arise from the test operation: ·3 for the 350 level and ·7 for the 400 level itself.

The figures in this table are the expectations which would come into operation after the test launch had been analysed, and then one figure only would be applicable, and the others become void, depending on the value indicated by the test.

A short-cut method

Now it becomes possible, using this set of results obtained directly from Figure 3.6, to take a short cut to the results obtained in Figure 3.9, with in most cases only a small sacrifice in statistical logic or accuracy. The argument, slightly spurious as it is, runs as follows.

Prior to the projectable test launch the final result of any testing is still unknown – whether it will provide an estimate of 200 or 400 cases of sales or whatever. There are, however, the assessed probabilities of the likelihood of any of the levels of achievement being met in the market, and it is assumed that these can also be used as approximate estimates of the probability of getting the various test results. The assessed probabilities are therefore applied to the calculated expectations to get an assessment of the overall expectation of profits after testing.

Post-test level	Expectation	Probability	Pre-post expectation
150	0	·10	0
200	0	·25	0
250	45	·30	13·5
300	145	·20	29·0
350	245	·10	24·5
400	340	·05	17·0
		1·00	84·0

The levels of 150 and 200 cases of achievement have both been given expectations of zero, since in the event of these readings being obtained from the test, the company would not go ahead with the product on an unprofitable basis and thus the theoretical losses would be avoided.

Overall, this method shows an expectation, after testing and obtaining more information about the likely outcome of the launch, of 84 units of profit emanating from the venture, which may be compared with the figure of 83·75 from the more rigorous method of calculation. Again, this is 44 more units than the best level which could have been expected without a projectable test launch, and this is a measure of 'benefit' to be set against the costs of conducting the test.

Interpretation of the matrices

The arithmetic can be extended to assess the profitability of other options open to the company, while examination of the matrices may in itself suggest alternative courses of action. For example, in Figure 3.7 planning on a basis of 200 cases provides an expectation of 40 units of profit. The current expectation after a test launch is completed is 84 units of profit. The cost of testing will consist largely of loss of profits for several months while the test is completed, and in this situation it may be possible to consider other options than small area testing or immediate launching, given sufficient flexibility in production and so on. It might, for example, be possible to consider producing on the 200-case basis and launching in half the country or in some form of rolling launch. Here the company is accepting some risk that even 200 cases capacity may be excessive and lead to losses. On the other hand, if the product is successful, the costs of testing will have been reduced by only keeping the product out of half the country rather than out of 95 per cent of it. This problem will be referred to again in Chapter 5.

The procedures outlined above provide a workable basis for assessing whether to test launch or not. Even if all the data needed for full calculation are not available, knowledge of the method may still be useful in arriving at decisions.

As with all numerical aids used in moving towards decisions, the results should be looked at very carefully indeed before being put into use, and tests should be made of the 'robustness' of the answer. This is usually done by altering some of the variables entering into the calculations, and observing the effect on the answers. In this case, assuming the costings are soundly based, there is no point in varying the profit or loss figures in the matrix. On the other hand, the probabilities have been derived from some mixture of measurements based on pre-testing, analysis of market data, and experience, and are at best only approximate. Hence it is wise to work out the results again, using a slightly different, but still appropriate, set of probabilities.

If the result of changing the probabilities by the widest margins by which they might be wrong does not change the decision (i.e. to test or launch or abandon, etc.), the system is 'robust' and the decision needs no qualification. If, however, the result of changing the probabilities only slightly is to produce results which lead to different decisions, such as from launching directly to test launching, the system is not robust enough for complete reliance to be placed on the results, and more data – from testing – is needed.

Bayesian statistics

The methods outlined above are based on principles originally developed by the Rev. Thomas Bayes in the eighteenth century. His work was largely ignored until a few years ago, when its value in enabling subjective or objective expectations to be built into decision-making processes began to be appreciated.

Those familiar with the normal methods of Bayesian statistics will realize that some of the usual sequence of steps have been omitted from the procedures described here. This is possible since it is assumed that the probability attached to each level of achievement can be applied irrespective of the planning level; and that a single set of values can be applied to the probabilities that the results of test launching will be high or low, irrespective of the actual value recorded. In most cases, in the state of knowledge in which such calculations are made, these assumptions can be accepted, but where there is doubt about their validity the services of a statistician in sympathy with the Bayesian approach should be sought.

Since decision-making processes abound in marketing, application of the methods is by no means limited to the specific case of test launching a new product discussed here. It is also possible to take the application a good deal farther in some cases involving a wider range of factors and their probabilities and possibly involving simulation techniques so as to arrive at any solution.

Not infrequently the lack of relevant data may impose limitations on the extent to which the method can be used, but even in these cases some knowledge of an underlying structure on which a decision might be based is often a useful adjunct to disciplined thinking.

4

When to use market testing

Experiments involving market testing of changes in factors associated with existing products fall into two broad categories:

1 Experiments to determine whether some specific alternative to an existing programme will be beneficial, with a view to accepting or rejecting the proposal.
2 Experiments to explore the relationship between selected factors and sales or profits, so as to be able to assess whether any change towards an optimal, or at least an improved, level is indicated.

The marketing factors associated with an existing product which are controlled by a company, and which can therefore be changed experimentally, also fall into two categories:

1 Factors where a change normally involves innovation or development, and a definite movement from one alternative to another, as in packaging, the content of the advertising, or the range of media used. Changes in this category will be called innovations.
2 Factors where, within reasonable limits, there is scope for variation, including such factors as price, trade terms, the length of journey cycles, and the advertising appropriation or the way it is divided between currently used media. Changes in this category will be called variations.

Specific versus exploratory experiments

Innovations normally lead to specific experiments. Where there are alternative candidates for selection, such as a number of potential new pack designs or a number of possible new campaigns, some form of pre-testing will normally be used to select the most promising before market testing as such is considered. The market test therefore is normally specific, to determine whether a new idea is better than existing ones; even where two or more alternatives are finally tested, the tests remain separate and specific.

Where variation is possible in a factor, either category of experiment may be undertaken, according to objectives and conditions. The relationship between price and sales, for example, might be explored experimentally by changing the price in selected areas and measuring sales and profits. Under suitable conditions, it could then become possible to analyse and quantify the relationship and to use this to determine the optimum price which will maximize profits. Alternatively, if a company is under pressure to raise prices, but is dubious about the effect of this on sales and has no knowledge of the type of relationship involved, then it would be possible to mount a specific test to assess the effect of the proposed new price level.

These differences between testing innovations on a go, no-go basis and attempting to find relationships so as to set variable factors at their most profitable levels call not only for differences in the design and execution of experiments, but, more importantly, seem to demand two different philosophies.

Experiments with innovations, including incidentally new products, are generally defensive, aimed more often at avoiding failure or loss than at the maximization of benefits, though clearly any innovation will only be considered in the first place in expectation of some benefit. With changes of degree, however, the whole object of experiment becomes to search for benefits beyond those enjoyed in an existing situation. These are essentially aggressive, seeking to find the levels at which various existing marketing activities should be set so as to obtain the maximum overall benefit.

While many companies have already adopted the more defensive philosophies leading to test launching and the market testing of specific alternatives, comparatively few have as yet developed those more positive and creative philosophies which question every aspect of their existing marketing practice and which may lead to almost continuous experimentation to maximize benefits. Companies which demand rigorous testing in innovation are still slow to experiment with such variable factors as the level of their advertising appropriation and the use to which it is put, the organization of their sales force, prices, or other similar factors. Yet in other aspects of their operations – in their production processes, for example – they may well be following such a policy.

In most marketing situations these variable factors will almost certainly have reached some satisfactory level of operation, but it is unlikely that they will all have gravitated to the optimum level at any one time, or that optimum levels will continue unchanged as marketing conditions change. Experimental work will often therefore show up certain areas in which improvements can be made by moving in either one direction or another. Because there are numbers of such factors, extensive planning and control is necessary if unambiguously beneficial results are to be achieved, and this process will be helped considerably if some 'model' of the market, however simple or rudimentary, is first developed.

Marketing models

A full discussion of marketing models is outside the scope of this book but a brief description and explanation may be useful. A marketing model sets out to describe how a market operates, and how the basic factors which can be manipulated by a company – advertising expenditure, the sales organization, price, distribution, etc. – affect the final levels of sales and profitability. In a fully developed form it will show both the mechanisms by which the factors become effective as well as the extent to which changes in these factors affect the outcome. Such a model will not merely show where relationships exist between input factors and output, but will also provide some statistical basis for assessing the effects on output of variations in inputs.

In some markets there may be direct, simple relationships between a particular factor and sales, as, for example, in a market where price is of prime importance. In other cases, and these are probably more numerous, factors do not act singly in so simple a fashion, but their effects are inter-related; changes in distribution, for example, may only be effective if given sufficient advertising support, or an increase in advertising expenditure may only be effective if given a sufficient level of distribution.

Since the objective in building models of markets is to be able to quantify these relationships, the models take the form of series of equations which both specify the nature of the relationships and define the extent of the effects produced. The complexity of these equations may call for the use of a computer if effective use is to be made of the models.

A model is built up through the careful study and analysis of available past data covering the marketing inputs of both the product concerned as well as its competitors and the effects on sales and profitability. Initially, models are likely to be rather crude and imprecise, since the shape of past events or records of past performance have seldom been organized in a way suitable for this new purpose. Once a start has been made, however, every new change, and particularly every new experiment, can be made to yield data to improve the model.

The factors which can enter most easily into a model are those which can be represented in quantitative terms, such as an advertising appropriation of £x, the price of y pennies, or distribution in z per cent of effective outlets. Given the necessary data, the relationships between these factors and sales or profits can be established. When other factors are considered, such as the packaging or the content of the advertising, these cannot at this stage be given any numerical value and so it is difficult to place them usefully in a model. Where innovations have been introduced in the past, then it is often possible to establish the effects of each event such as changes in packaging or advertising content; but such results merely record historically the effects of one alternative, and no amount of historical data is likely to enable the model to predict the effects of a new, untried, and unmeasured innovation.

In time, if methods of pre-testing packages, campaigns, etc., can be developed to show a predictable relationship between the results of pre-testing and the effects on sales levels, then these factors can be built into quantified marketing models. However, this is not possible at this early stage of investigation, and models remain more useful for dealing with the 'variable' aspects of marketing rather than with those factors which change by innovation. Which brings us back to our original division of factors under the company's control.

Benefits of models

A number of benefits follow from having such a model, even if it is only in a rudimentary or unquantified state, for it brings together in a compact and retrievable form the results of past experience; the simple attempt to develop a model of a market will high-light areas where experience is lacking and where exploratory experiments might be carried out with advantage. For example, in some markets price may have remained static for a long period, and there may then be insufficient data to establish any relationship between price and sales from existing data; alternatively, if all brands have previously changed their prices together and maintained their relative levels, no information on the effects of relative price changes can be fed into the model, and neither will any output be available. In such cases exploratory experiments may be indicated.

In other cases the data available may be sufficient to indicate the nature of relationships, but without generating a precise quantitative assessment of the magnitude of the relationship. Thus analysis of the effects of previous price rises may establish that additional profits have been made in each case, but it may not be possible to indicate how far prices could be raised before a fall-off in sales affected profits adversely. Again, a need for exploratory testing may be indicated.

With those more advanced models which have had the benefit of an ample supply of past variations and adequate measurements, more considerable advantages can be expected, since it then becomes possible to put questions to the model and to obtain quantified answers. It may, for instance, become possible to assess from the model the likely effects of a range of variations in price in terms of sales and profits. The need for any further exploration of the effects of price changes may thus be avoided altogether, all that is necessary being a specific experiment to confirm that the proposed change (to, presumably, a new optimum level) will yield the expected results. In time, if the projections made by the model in response to questions on price are consistently validated in the market, even this stage of specific testing may be omitted with a consequent saving in time and research costs.

A further benefit from having a model is that it will illuminate interactions between different factors and enable experiments to be planned more effectively. For example, there may well be some interaction between price, advertising expenditure, and sales. Simple experiments changing one factor at a time may show that increasing the price above the existing level reduces profits as a result of a fall in sales. Similar experiments may show that increasing the advertising expenditure is unprofitable since it will not attract sufficient additional sales to maintain profits. The model, however, while supporting these findings, may indicate that there is an interaction between these two factors, so that if both were increased together the outcome would be profitable. In this case, therefore, there would be no point in carrying out the single factor tests where all other factors are held constant, but considerable benefit from testing changes in both factors together. Such cases may not be uncommon where, for example, scope for advertising to attract new buyers is limited, but where increased effort might be beneficial in maintaining loyalty in the face of an increased price.

A model of a market is also useful in planning experiments by indicating the way in which the factors in a market operate to produce their effects. Thus it may be made easier in some cases to decide where measurements should most effectively be made, and so to yield the best balance between costs and information.

Models capable of offering all these types of assistance to marketing personnel contemplating change or experiment will take time and data to set up. But, once a start is made, experiments can be designed to contribute to the efficiency of the model, while, at the same time, the model should improve the efficiency of experiments by indicating in advance the magnitude of changes that will need to be measured and where in the system this can best be done. At present, however, few such models exist, and the discussion must return to the more basic problems of market experiments.

Analysis of existing data

Experience suggests that many experiments which have been carried out in the past, would not have been undertaken had more attention been paid to prior analysis of existing data and information. Even where such analysis could not have provided all the information needed for a final decision, it would often have given sufficient extra information for a more efficient experiment.

The experimenter or researcher is naturally at a disadvantage where dealing with a situation in a state of ignorance. Hence the researcher set a problem will almost certainly come back with a series of questions seeking information on which to plan the operation. Not infrequently, the answers may reveal gaps in the thinking which led to the decision to carry out a market test, and this may change the problem or even, in some cases, show that it does not exist.

'No change' experiments

Such a situation tends to occur where the object of the experiment is to discover whether a change can be made in a marketing factor without detriment. For example, might a saving be effected by dropping small accounts from lists of direct calls? Might a price be increased without losing sales volume? Might a cheaper ingredient be substituted, or used in increased quantities, without loss of sales? Here the hoped-for results, even if not technically the most likely, are that any downward changes in sales will be sufficiently small for the resulting profit to at least maintain the current level.

In most experimental situations it is impossible to determine that no change has taken place, for two reasons. First, a change may have occurred that is smaller than the measuring mechanism can detect, as in the analogy of attempting to measure the coefficient of expansion of a six-inch nail with a school ruler. (However often it is done, and however often a null result is obtained, it will still not be proved that a six-inch nail remains unchanged in size when heated.) Secondly, a change may have occurred in certain dimensions of the market which have not been measured. For example, measurements of sales out of shops taken off a list of direct calls may show no change for some months afterwards, but the attitude of the retailers towards the company may have changed in a way which may later make them more susceptible to the introduction of a competitive product.

Closer examination of cases where the apparent objective is to change marketing factors without changing sales generally will show that there is an alternative way of formulating the objectives so as to avoid the impossible research task of proving nothing has changed. The gain to the company of making the changes is quantifiable in cost terms, just as the costs of increasing marketing activity are quantifiable. The key figure is the extent of the saving to be expected if nothing else changes. If a successful change could save the company $£x$ or $\$y$, then the research will be adequate and the experiment can proceed so long as the means of measurement are capable of measuring changes in sales which correspond to changes in profits of this order. Then, if no change is observed in the results, it becomes possible to report that even though some change may have taken place, it is not large enough to wipe out all the benefits and some residual benefit will be left to the company.

In some cases the mere calculations of the limits of change may be sufficient to solve the problem completely, as the following case history involving the brand leader in a large market shows. The problem was posed in the following terms (suitably disguised).

'We need to increase our prices by 10 per cent. We cannot consider any lower figure because of difficulties in pricing and trade terms, and any higher figure is out of the question. We are afraid that the price increase might lead to lower sales, but we hope not. Can you set up a test operation so that we can see whether or not sales fall?'

The first problem was clearly to discover how far sales could fall at the new price and leave profits unchanged. Surprisingly, this had not been worked out, yet apart from any other considerations it was necessary in planning effective research to know whether a drop of x per cent in sales would be critical, or whether the critical level was much lower.

Obviously sales revenue could be maintained or improved provided sales volume did not drop below about 90 per cent of the existing level. It then transpired that the company was afraid sales might fall to this level and that turnover would suffer. This was a start, but the real problem was how far sales volume could fall before the whole increased profit from the price rise would be lost. This is a simple problem, and the answer depends on the ratio between the direct costs of producing the product at a given level of output (normally the costs of materials and labour) and the fixed costs (including here all selling and advertising expenses).

The calculations involved could be reduced to a simple formula, which, while it may not be completely accurate from a cost accounting angle, is generally adequate to provide a first approximation in such cases.

Let Q = quantity being sold now (per week, month, etc.)
P = current price
a = fixed costs
b = direct costs per unit
q = quantity sold at new price
p = new price
k = current profit

Under the existing price structure, the profit, k, is given by:

$$k = Q.P - a - Q.b$$

To achieve the same profit, k, under the new price, p, it is necessary for the new quantity, q, to fit the equation:

$$k = q.p - a - q.b$$

Hence, since k remains equal, the minimum profit condition is given by:

$$Q.P - a - Q.b = q.p - a - q.b$$

Rearranging and simplifying the equation, the new quantity required as a minimum to maintain the level of profit at k is:

$$q = Q.\frac{P - b}{p - b}$$

Here the fixed costs have cancelled out, since they must still be met at the same level, the new quantity depending on the differences between the old and new prices and the direct costs of producing one unit. If the two quantities, Q and q, are very different, then there may be changes in the direct costs and this must be allowed for in the denominator. However, the object of the operation is not to calculate a precise figure below which sales must not fall if profits are to be preserved, but merely to gain some idea of the 'shape' of the problem involved.

In the problem posed above, the calculations were made by the accountants in the manufacturing company, and they arrived at an answer of 82 per cent of the existing level. This figure changed the nature of the problem and all its implications, because while there were real fears that sales at the new price might fall to 90 per cent of the existing level, no one in the organization believed that they were likely to drop to 82 per cent if the price was raised by 10 per cent. In arriving at this conclusion, of course, a wide range of factors was considered, including not only the reaction of customers, but also the reactions of the trade and of competitors in the market.

As all the expected levels of achievement after the price rise were now more profitable than the existing level of operations, there was no point in testing to ensure that the outcome would be profitable. Testing would merely delay the realization of the increased profits for as long as it took to mount and assess the test – probably between six and twelve months.

The disturbing factor here was that the figures had not been calculated by the company before they sought a test operation. The thinking that had gone into the project had been concerned with the effect on the volume of sales and not on the level of profits that would be achieved. Under certain circumstances, volume may well be a factor, as, for example, with packaged goods moving through supermarkets when loss of volume may mean loss of shelf-space or of distribution, but even here it is only important because a fall may have a snowballing effect, and thus adversely affect profits. It is a fault of the way in which certain companies are organized that executives at brand levels may either be briefed to regard volume as their objective, or else they just drift into this attitude and ignore the profit factor.

In less clear-cut cases, where the result is not the abandonment of testing, these calculations help to provide a framework within which the economics and cost-effectiveness of testing can be assessed. This is done in a way similar to that discussed for projectable test launching, combining the profits or losses at each possible level of achievement with assessments of the likelihood of that level occurring.

The precision of measurements

A second set of factors already mentioned are those concerned with the precision with which results can be measured. This subject will be discussed in more detail in Chapter 9, but it is also appropriate to comment on it here, since it is unfortunate that some of the effects which may be produced in experiment can be too small to be measured accurately or even detected by the use of existing market research techniques on any practicable scale.

Consider a branded product bought by, say, 20 per cent of housewives during a three-month period, or by 30 per cent during a six-month period. Measurements of the numbers of buyers among a panel of 1,000 housewives in a simple test would need to show a rise from 20 to about 23 per cent from one quarter to another before it could be firmly assumed that the level had changed at all and that the results were not merely due to chance fluctuations. Expressed in terms of the number of housewives buying the brand in a quarter, this is equivalent to a rise of 14 per cent. Consequently, the chance of obtaining an effective direct measurement of the results of an offer designed to increase the numbers of buyers in a quarter by, say, 10 per cent is not good, and there is therefore little hope of deciding in the short term whether or not the offer has reached its objective.

Fortunately, in most cases, the assessment of results can be extended over longer periods than a single quarter, either because the experimental stimulus is present for longer or because its effects are more long-lasting. There may also be more than a single set of measurements available from which to draw inferences, or it may become possible to use deeper types of analysis, so leading to a more precise identification of results. However, in the same way as attempts to measure the coefficient of expansion of a six-inch nail with a school ruler will fail so must some constraint be accepted about the size of results measurable with existing market research tools.

In practice, this constraint means that some assessment of the outcome must be made before embarking on an experiment, in terms either of what can reasonably be expected or of what is minimally necessary for the proposals to be profitable. In many cases there may be considerable confusion between what can reasonably be expected and what is hoped for, but there should be no great difficulty in determining the level of change necessary to cover any increased operating costs. This then becomes the vital figure, and only if ways of measuring to these limits are available and will yield results within an acceptable time, should the test normally proceed.

With exploratory experiments it is often possible to avoid the restrictions imposed by the precision of research facilities by exaggerating the changes in the variables being examined. If the advertising appropriation is being changed so as to assess the general effect on levels of sales, then more satisfactory results will usually be achieved if the intervals between the levels tested are large; changes in sales are then also likely to be large and to be measurable without undue effort and without being subject to undue doubts about their validity. Large changes of this nature may be outside the range which can be considered for adoption on a wider scale, and to that extent an element of artificiality is introduced into the experiments, but some movement at least should be observable. If only small changes are used in line with what would be practicable on a larger scale, the movements may be too small to be measured with any useful degree of certainty. On balance, it is generally better to have widely spaced but firm results, while interpolating the likely effects of smaller changes, than to have in-conclusive results about the outcome of the smaller changes themselves.

The time factor

There is a third factor which has a bearing on this type of experimenta-tion, and that is the quite considerable time which may be required for the effects of changes to become evident in research results. Cost and time will in certain cases remain closely linked anyway, but even if the experiment is costing nothing time may still be a vital factor.

A number of examples need to be considered. The first occurs where an experiment involves some strengthening or addition to marketing activity, such as an increase in appropriation or additions to a sales force. Here a lack of positive results over one whole season or year will generally provide valid grounds for abandoning the experiment and a time-limit can quite reasonably be set when the experiment is planned.

A different case arises when similar experiments, involving increases in marketing factors, rapidly show positive results of a magnitude sufficient to justify their adoption on a wider scale. Here it is normally essential to continue the experiment for sufficient time to ensure that any subsequent decay in the effects will still yield a profitable level of improvement. Further, even after the change has been adopted more widely, measurements should continue to be maintained in the original test areas until any fears of decay can be finally dismissed.

The situation tends to be more difficult in experiments where effort is diminished, as in cutting an appropriation or decreasing direct selling activity. Particularly with well-established products, the effects even of radical changes may take a long time to work through the system and appear in results. In one such highly competitive market, experiments were conducted varying the level of the advertising appropriation. Television was the only medium being used by the brand concerned, and this was dropped completely in two areas while being maintained at normal levels elsewhere. Even with this marked change in marketing strategy, it was a full fifteen months before the brand share of the product moved, when it fell precipitously. Subsequent heavy expenditure was necessary to bring sales levels up again in these two areas, and it would clearly have been wrong to have stopped this experiment after even twelve months when there was still no apparent effect.

This last example, which is only slightly unusual, even though such a marked result was delayed for so long, indicates another aspect of this type of research. The result showed that ceasing to advertise for fifteen months would lead to a drastic reduction in sales and in profits. Such a finding, however, raises the possibility of a number of other variations in the appropriation which it might be possible and profitable to pursue. What, for example, would have happened if advertising at the normal level had been restarted after twelve months? Would the sales level have been held without any fluctuation, or would there still have been a marked decline in sales at some later date. If twelve months is too long a period during which to stop advertising, because ultimately there would be a drop in sales, can it be stopped for nine months, six months, or even three months without any apparent long-term effect? In another dimension, one is led to ponder the possible effects of doubling the weight of advertising for a period and then stopping for an equivalent period and perhaps following a wave pattern of advertising, not necessarily within the usual restrictions of a season or a financial year, but on a much longer-term basis.

Clearly, to experiment in this area will take considerable periods of time, since an experiment in which advertising is stopped for twelve months and then restarted could not be expected to give a definite conclusion on the effect on the sales curve for at least eighteen months, and a two-year period would be preferable. The point to emphasize is the need for a proper experimental plan so that possible alternative and beneficial variations in the marketing factors can be introduced into other areas as soon as the existing experiments indicate that their outcome might be favourable. In this particular instance, it was not at any point foreseen that it might take fifteen months for the market to show signs of declining, but in subsequent experiments one would now tend to seek agreement to a plan which might involve stopping advertising in three or four areas together, and reintroducing it after three months, six months, or twelve months if the sales line with no advertising showed no change. Thus when, after fifteen months, the group of experiments had arrived at the point where a change could be expected, parallel results would have been available to show the effects of stoppages in advertising for three months, six months and twelve months respectively.

When to use exploratory experiments

To say that exploratory experiments should be undertaken 'whenever possible' implies that there are certain constraints, and the first of these may be cost. These costs may arise in setting up the experimental situations, as when increasing the pressure of advertising in an area, or in measuring the results through market research. Research costs can often be reduced, or even eliminated, by making full use of area data which may already be available from existing sales analysis, store audits, consumer panels or consumer surveys.

A range of experiments can often be carried out without any additional commitment on the part of the company, and these include experiments in the spacing of a given appropriation through time – wave or burst advertising of various forms as against continuous advertising – the use of peak-time against off-peak or variations in allocation of appropriation between different media. Experiments on the level of the total appropriation can often be carried out by increasing the appropriation in one area and dropping it in another, so leaving the total expenditure unchanged while allowing useful experimentation on two levels.

Such experiments, carried out in areas already separately measured and reported on within the basic research programme, often show results which lead to beneficial changes in media scheduling without involving additional expenditure. They have also been the means by which companies have been encouraged to adopt or develop a more positive policy of market testing involving other aspects of marketing, and where experimentation unavoidably costs money.

When to use specific experiments

Specific experiments to assess whether an innovation or a change to a particular new level of a variable factor should be introduced into a wider market must be examined at four levels before any decision is taken.

First, there should be an assessment of the limits within which the experiment can be considered successful. If additional costs are involved how far must sales increase to cover these and leave profits unchanged? If costs will fall, how far can sales fall before the whole saving is lost and profits suffer? If a specific increase in profits is sought of £x or \$$x$ or y per cent, what level of sales is needed to produce this, taking into account other changes in costs? Questions of this type, adapted to the specific experiment, can and must be answered from data within the company if the break-even points in the system are to be identified.

Secondly, the chances of sales (or whatever the measure of effect being used) moving to these levels must be assessed. With innovations, this must depend heavily on experience and the interpretation of pre-testing results. With variations, it may prove possible to use an existing model of a market or to establish some usable relationship between the level of the variable and sales from past data so as to obtain a statistical projection of the likely outcome which may be used as a basis for such an assessment. If the assessment shows that the chances of a fall in profits can be ignored, or that there is no hope of avoiding a fall, then there is no point in experimenting. Where assessment shows some chance of success and some of failure, the probabilities of various levels of achievement can be assessed as for a single row of the project-able test-launching matrix.

Thirdly, how accurately can the effects be measured through some form of research, and at what cost, and how long must the experiment run?

Fourthly, where a clear decision has not already emerged from the previous three stages, the probabilities of various levels of achievement, the profits and losses involved, and the costs of experimenting need to be brought together, as in projectable test-launching, to determine the cost-benefit implications of abandoning the project, or experimenting, or proceeding directly to a wider market.

With exploratory research a similar logical approach is needed. The possible subjects for research, even in a simple marketing operation, will certainly indicate more possible experiments than a company is capable of mounting at any one time, and so some initial assessments of the potential benefits of investigating the various areas will be necessary.

Whether or not an experiment involves direct costs and whether it is specific or exploratory, it should only be undertaken after it has become quite clear that the additional information it will yield will be positively beneficial and that no comparable information can be obtained more cheaply or quickly from back-data or other sources.

5

The scale of experiments

The scale on which an experiment is carried out tends to be determined by three sets of factors whose relative importance varies between one experiment and another. These are:

1 The constraints imposed by the conditions and nature of the experiment itself.
2 The facilities needed to provide research of an acceptable level of precision.
3 The financial considerations.

The nature of an experiment and its research requirements usually impose lower limits to the scale, below which an experiment of the type and the precision envisaged will not be possible. Financial aspects normally tend to set upper limits to the scale, above which it would be imprudent or impossible for the company to operate the experiment.

Physical limitations

The lower limits imposed by the nature of the experiment itself may be trivial, or they may indicate that only a large-scale experiment is at all practicable. In a feasibility test on sales of an exotic imported food, for example, the lower limit may be only a single shop. A single supermarket may be all that is needed for a simple experiment on the effects of a new dump-bin, a banded pack, or an on-pack offer. These are not necessarily acceptable lower limits from the research aspects, which will depend on the use to be made of the results and the precision required, but they may well be the only limits set by simple experiments of this kind.

Conversely, the lower limits set by experiments involving main advertising media will be much larger. They will be geared to the smallest circulation or transmission areas covered by suitable publications or transmitters. With VHF television in Great Britain, this has in the past meant that the minimum size of experiments involving television has been an area including upwards of half a million people, although the provision of suitable switching facilities in conjunction with VHF transmitters may change this situation in the future. In markets where research facilities can utilize community antennae with split cables, or where 'Ad-Lab' facilities, like those in Milwaukee, are available, it becomes possible to mount quite complex comparative experiments on a much smaller scale. These developments are discussed further in Chapter 12.

Other limiting factors arising from the nature of the experiment are the size of sales territories, the coverage of local depots, the nature of the distribution system, or the need to provide a market for a certain minimum production capacity. An experiment to change the journey cycle may call for the amalgamation of four territories into three, or the expansion of four into five, and this may set a lower limit. It may be impracticable to have an existing and an experimentally relaunched product passing through the same depot simultaneously, and so the size of the experiment is governed by the capacity of the smallest depot. If wholesalers are used, particularly if they are cash-and-carry outlets, experiments involving the product, packaging, price, promotions, etc., must normally be carried out in areas which can be reasonably well isolated and which then tend to be of some size. Or if some fraction of productive or packaging capacity has to be converted for the experiment, it may be necessary to provide an area to absorb the goods produced if shortages of existing production are not to occur.

Whichever of these, or other similar factors associated with the experiment, sets the highest minimum condition will determine the smallest scale of experimentation acceptable for this group of factors.

Research factors

Research requirements will also tend to set certain lower limits to the scale of an experiment, and they in turn will depend on the objectives and the degree of precision required in the results. Sometimes the same type of experiment may be repeated with different specific objectives, and this will lead to variations in the minimum acceptable scale for meeting the research requirements. Thus a company considering a display stand for distribution to retailers may as a first step decide to test the broad effects of the stand by using a few prototypes before becoming committed to any larger production order. In such a situation a small-scale test, using perhaps only half a dozen stores, would probably be enough to ensure that the device has some merit and is worth proceeding with in a wider test. If this wider test is then to produce a reasonable assessment of the number of retailers who might accept the stand and of the effect it might have on sales, in order that the costs of national distribution and the likely additional sales can be compared, then a much larger sample of retailers must be utilized. Clearly, if the number required in the sample is, say, 100, and if the particular type of shop concerned exists in the ratio of one to every 3,000 people, a city or area containing at least 300,000 people will be required. Allowing for possible refusals among retailers to co-operate in the research by, for example, refusing to allow their stocks to be audited, the minimum planning area may become 400,000 people or more.

Research among people normally imposes fewer limitations than research among retailers or other establishments, unless exceptionally restricted sectors of the population are involved. Hence minimum limits are likely to be lower when only consumer research – whether through ad hoc surveys or continuous panels – is needed than when store audits are required.

The research requirements may impose limitations on scale in another dimension, however, since the mere availability of adequate numbers of stores or people may not be sufficient to achieve the research objectives. Thus a city of 400,000 people may be large enough to supply a sample of 100 stores of the kind required, but it will still be inadequate for the research if there is reason to believe that retailers or their customers may behave differently in large as against small communities, or in rural districts rather than in urban areas, or in communities in different geographical areas. A more detailed discussion of this subject is left until Chapter 6, but clearly the research requirements may lead not merely to demands for some minimum scale, but for more detailed specification of the type of area required and possibly for the provision of more than one area.

The discussion has so far assumed that the experiment is a simple one, with only one possible course of action or project being tested. Where alternatives are being tested, as with two or three different levels of advertising in a pressure test, then in general separate minimum areas are needed for testing each alternative. In some cases careful consideration of the problem may suggest ways of reducing the scale of a project, as when testing combinations of television with either press, couponing or sampling, where if the television element is to be kept constant then all three variations may be tested in separate towns within a single television area. Hence, under favourable circumstances, the minimum scale for the three tests together may be no larger than for any single test separately, provided, of course, that the towns are large enough to meet the research requirements.

Financial factors

The third set of factors that may impose constraints on the scale of an experiment are the financial considerations. Not infrequently these take the form of a more or less arbitrarily imposed budget covering some, all, or even an unspecified part, of the costs involved. Sometimes the budget is set on the research costs, sometimes on advertising and research costs combined, sometimes on the advertising expenditure alone, which is then raided for whatever research expenditure is deemed necessary. Seldom is much real consideration given to the nature of the costs involved with a view to achieving the required results most economically. As a result, some tests are excessively large, having been geared to an unnecessarily high budget. Others are restricted to a scale which, even though completely successful as a test, costs the company more than a *larger* experiment would have done, and which, the risks involved being considered, it would have been justified in mounting.

While the scale of an experiment is generally linked to the cost of carrying it out, it is not necessarily linked in any simple way, and in any logical approach to the problem different types of costs which all behave differently must be considered. Basically, three main types can be distinguished, and these may be called (a) the out-of-pocket expenses, (b) opportunity costs, and (c) pull-out costs.

Out-of-pocket expenses

The out-of-pocket expenses are the ordinary costs of organizing, mounting, and measuring the experiment, and they are the sums of money which the company will have to spend if the experiment is to be carried out at all. Certain cases may involve no out-of-pocket expenses, as, for example, when current advertising material is used in an area which is already broken out in continuous research to run an experimental new schedule within the current appropriation. It follows in this case that the size of the area chosen has no effect on the out-of-pocket expenses, and these then cease to be a factor in determining the scale of the experiment.

In other situations, the out-of-pocket expenses may be heavy, and some care may be needed to form a proper assessment. If a new product is to be test launched prior to deciding whether or not to proceed to a national scale, there may be costs of plant, raw materials, labour, packaging, advertising, production costs, and media costs. Any revenue expected from sales in the test area should be set against these costs, and subsequent calculations will be simplified if this is assessed on the assumption that the test will achieve the minimum level of success.

If a new product is to be pilot launched between the decision to launch nationally and the time when it becomes physically possible to do so, using, perhaps, a pilot plant, or the first of a series of production lines being built to supply anticipated national demand, the out-of-pocket expenses may be considerably reduced. This follows because the test would be using such items as package designs and advertising material to which the company is already committed, having taken the decision to market nationally in time.

Precisely what is to be included may vary from one company to another, but the basic question is how much will the company spend during the experiment which it would not have spent without the experiment? For a company which seldom undertakes marketing experiments, the details may be settled as each case arises, but if there is much experimentation, clearly a great deal of time and discussion can be saved if an agreed policy has been worked out between those involved. The sort of problem which arises, for example, and to which different companies may give different answers, are whether the costs of the sales force or head office executives are to be included. Some companies argue that the test is incidental to other duties for which the staff would have received their salaries anyway, and that the test has added nothing to the salary bill. Other companies argue that some part of these salaries is a fair charge against the test and must be considered as an out-of-pocket expense.

A feature which commonly distinguishes out-of-pocket expenses from opportunity costs and pull-out costs is that, once defined, they can normally be assessed fairly accurately before the test is commenced, and that once an experiment is undertaken, the company is largely committed to the costs. The other two types of cost may be less easily assessable until the experiment is over, and then only one of the two sets will be involved, depending on whether the company goes ahead with the innovation or change or whether it pulls out. Hence, at the time when the decision to mount an experiment is taken, they can only be estimated, and probabilities of the likelihood of each occurring must be assessed.

Opportunity costs

Opportunity costs arise if a company finds from an experiment that the proposed course of action is profitable, but that it has foregone profits in the rest of the market while the experiment was taking place in a limited area.

One company with a seasonal product ran an experimental campaign for a season in an area containing about 5 per cent of the population and generating about 5 per cent of its sales. The result of the experiment was to show that the new campaign lifted sales in the test area, and that on a national basis an increase of 20 per cent in profits would have been achieved. By testing (for which, incidentally, they had good reasons), the company had lost the opportunity of increasing its profits over the whole area outside the test for a year by 20 per cent, although it had secured increased profits from the 5 per cent experimental area. Thus about 95 per cent of the 20 per cent extra profit had been lost, and this was a cost of testing which could never be directly recovered. In ten years' time the company would only have the extra profits from nine years, and so on to the death of the product.

Opportunity costs do not necessarily arise. In the above example, if the subject of the test had been a promotion which could only be used once in any area, and for which there was no risk of pre-emption by a competitor, the tested idea could have been used profitably in the rest of the market during the next season and the extra profits would not have been lost but merely deferred. (While on a discounted cash-flow basis, profits next year are not as valuable as profits this year, and a cost can be put on any delay in earning them, for purposes of assessment prior to an experiment taking place, the margins of uncertainty are likely to be too wide to justify the introduction of such refinements.)

There may be no opportunity costs in pilot-launching a new product when this is done while waiting for production facilities to build up to a total market level. Then the company has no opportunity at that time to earn profits on a wider basis, and the delay in earning them is not attributable to any experimentation which may take place. It may, indeed, be argued that, if a company in this situation fails to pilot launch the product, or only does so on a scale much smaller than the available production would allow, it incurs as an opportunity cost any profits which might have been earned, or earned more quickly, in the test area.

The unique point about opportunity costs is that they decrease as the scale of the experiment increases, whereas both out-of-pocket expenses and pull-out costs tend to increase with scale. In the case of the company testing the new campaign, the opportunity costs would have been reduced proportionately if the experiment had covered 10, 20, or 50 per cent of the market. If it had been 'tested' on a national basis, the opportunity costs would have been zero, but in fact the assessed probability of success had not been high and the pull-out costs had been too large to justify this risk.

The total costs of running an experiment which is successful and which leads to a company adopting a project are the out-of-pocket expenses plus the opportunity costs. For some purposes, these costs can be considered together, but for others it is useful to maintain the distinction between the two parts, not least because the former have to be met from existing resources, while the latter are resources which the company never obtains. The ultimate effect on the profit-and-loss account is, however, the same.

Pull-out costs

Pull-out costs are better considered in an opposite way to the costs of success, in that it is easier to define the total costs of failure and then to divide them into out-of-pocket expenses and net or residual pull-out costs. Since the calculation of out-of-pocket expenses allows for revenue from the minimum level of success, a lower level achieved in the event of failure is automatically included in the net pull-out costs.

Two main types of situation tend to arise with regard to pull-out costs. In the case of 'go, no-go' experiments, where subsequent decisions depend on the outcome, the decision to experiment at all will normally have been taken against the option of abandoning the project without testing. If the project is then abandoned after testing, the full pull-out costs should logically include all expenditure incurred between the two decisions, plus any subsequent cleaning-up costs and less anything that can be salvaged.

In the second type of situation, where an experiment is merely taking place within a process of development and marketing to which the company is already committed – as when a pilot launch is undertaken using pilot plant facilities while the main plant is being built – the pull-out costs will merely be any additional expenses incurred in organizing and supplying the experimental area ahead of the main launch. The pull-out would normally then be only from a marketing mix which had failed to come up to expectations and for which another would be substituted, and not a pull-out from the main project.

In some cases, there are no apparent pull-out costs, as when experimenting with the spacing or timing of advertisements within an existing budget, and even if the experiment merely leaves sales as they would otherwise have been, there are no residual pull-out costs if the idea is abandoned. If, however, the experiment should result in sales below normal, the potential loss of profits becomes a pull-out cost, as do the costs of any remedial action needed to restore the situation.

The more optimistic may be inclined to regard the outcome of an experiment on a project which fails in terms of the saving to the company from having limited its losses to the test area instead of incurring the larger losses of a wider failure. This, however, does not help to determine the scale appropriate to an experiment, though considered in conjunction with the opportunity costs involved in a successful experimental project it does lead to an interesting paradox: that while a successful experiment costs a company money, an unsuccessful experiment saves it.

Probabilities and expectations

The three types of experimental cost have a bearing on the scale appropriate to an experiment when linked to their respective probabilities of being incurred. At this stage, if the out-of-pocket expenses are kept separate, the probability of their being incurred if the experiment is undertaken at all is 100 per cent. Alternatively, if out-of-pocket expenses are added to opportunity costs and net pull-out costs so as to give total costs of success or failure, then they still have a probability within the equations of 100 per cent, provided the sum of the two probabilities of success or failure equals 100 per cent.

Consider a company contemplating test-launching a new product with a view to taking a 'go, no-go' decision, with an expectation p that the test will be successful, and an expectation q that it will fail. Assuming that one of the results will occur, then:

$$p + q = 1 \text{ (or 100\%)}$$

Then if:

$$x = \text{the level of out-of-pocket expenses}$$
$$y = \text{the assessed opportunity cost}$$
$$z = \text{the assessed net pull-out cost}$$

the prior expectation is that the test will cost E, where:

$$E = x + py + qz$$

Within this situation, the costs that will be incurred if the test is a success will be s, where:

$$s = x + y$$

and the cost of failure will be f, where:

$$f = x + z$$

Since E depends on the costs and probabilities of success or failure, the equation for E may be rewritten as:

$$E = ps + qf$$
$$= p(x + y) + q(x + z)$$
$$= py + qz + x(p + q)$$

Since $p + q = 1$, this is the original equation for E, showing that the same expectation is obtained whether out-of-pocket expenses are kept separate or whether they are included in total costs of success or failure.

The cost of success consists, in part, of the out-of-pocket expenses which a company must find in cash or credit, and, in part, of the opportunity costs, which, though they are lost to the company and decrease its profits below what might otherwise have been achieved, do not have to be found in this way. On the other hand, both components of the cost of failure – out-of-pocket expenses and any residual pull-out costs – have to be found from cash or credit. It is therefore wise to look first at the magnitude of the costs of failure in planning any experimentation.

Costs and scale

There will normally be some upper limit to the amount which a company can afford to risk in pull-out costs without facing ruin. In some cases, as with some large conglomerates, this may be a very high figure, or it may be very low in the case of a small company suffering, perhaps, from shortage of capital or liquid resources. Whatever the figure, it sets a nominal upper limit to the scale of the experiment.

Not infrequently, and particularly where the risk of failure is high, management may not be willing to put this nominal limiting sum at risk, and a lower limit will be imposed which will further restrict the scale of the experiment. An initial step therefore is to assess how large an experiment is possible within this limit, and to consider it in the light of other relevant factors. There may be a clash between the limit imposed by finance and the minimum area acceptable on other grounds, as when an experiment involving some specific form of advertising cannot be mounted on a sufficient scale to cover the smallest acceptable media areas. Then the experiment, and possibly the project, must either be abandoned or else some other type of experiment has to be devised under modified conditions.

When the financial limit is high enough for the experiment to be carried beyond the minimum levels set by other relevant factors, the behaviour of the pull-out costs at levels between the upper and lower limits of scale should be examined in detail. There will normally be the basic costs without which no experiment could be carried out at all, but beyond this level pull-out costs may rise smoothly as the scale is increased to the permitted maximum, or they may rise irregularly.

Figure 5.1 Pull-out costs in testing

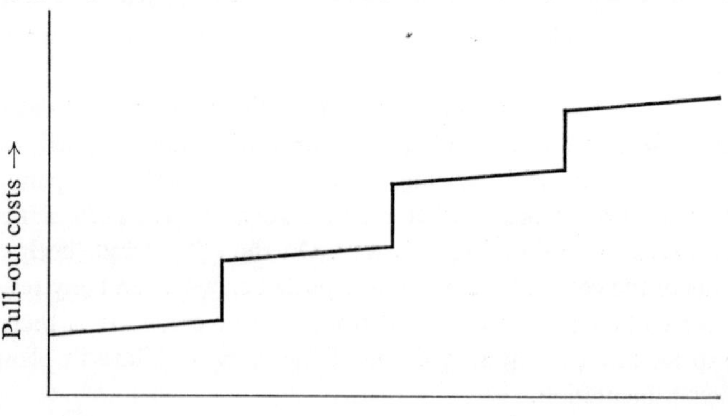

When pull-out costs rise in a series of steps, linked, perhaps, to the nature of the plant required for production at different levels, it may be found that they rise very little between an experiment covering an area containing, say, 200,000 people, and one containing, say, 500,000 people, but that they may immediately double if the population covered is increased to 550,000. This new level may then vary very little for covering a population up to 900,000, but then leap again if coverage is extended to a million. In such cases, when the pull-out costs are considered together with the opportunity costs and their associated probabilities, it will generally be found that the expectation of costs tends to be minimized when the experiment is scaled just smaller than a step in the pull-out cost curve, and that it becomes more 'expensive' to scale the experiment at other points on the flatter parts of the curve (see Figure 5.1).

Opportunity costs tend to decrease with the scale of experiments more smoothly than pull-out costs increase, since they depend more directly on the proportion of the wider market excluded from the experiment. Since these 'costs' do not have to be found in the same way as pull-out or out-of-pocket costs, there are generally fewer problems in dealing with them, but nevertheless attention should be paid

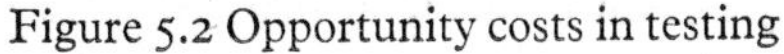

Figure 5.2 Opportunity costs in testing

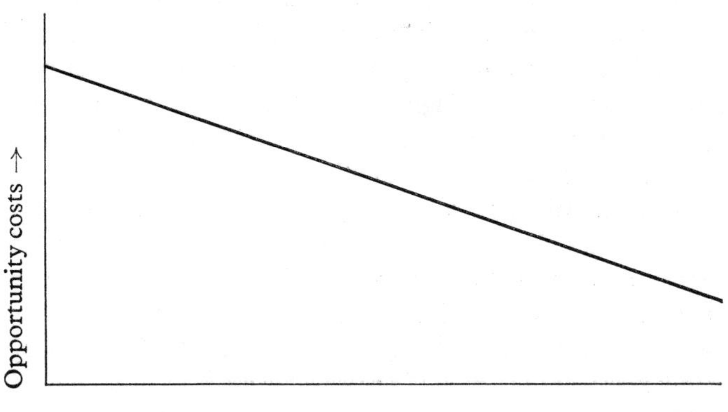

to their existence when experiments are planned. Where they have been ignored in the past many experiments have been conducted on an unprofitably small scale.

Out-of-pocket expenses tend to rise with the scale of an experiment, but two different sets of factors are at work. First there may be costs which tend to increase directly with scale, such as distribution costs or advertising. Secondly, there are such other costs as research costs, which will change only marginally as the scale is increased, unless there is also a change in the design of the experiment.

Scale and experimental design

The same basic measures could, for example, in many experiments be made in a town or area containing 500,000 people as economically as in one containing 200,000 people, but if the opportunity was taken in the larger option of using two areas of 200,000 people, then the research costs would generally double. Scale and design then become interrelated, and since out-of-pocket costs are part of the costs of both success and failure, separate assessments of the behaviour of pull-out costs with scale will be needed for each potential experimental design.

The aspects of scale linked to design become important if there should be wide variations in the acceptance of the new project in different areas of the wider market. This subject will be referred to again in Chapter 6, but the effect on scale warrants further discussion here.

If it is confidently expected that reaction to the new project will be uniform throughout the wider market, or at least highly correlated with some other factor already known by area, so that adequate projections can be made between areas, an experiment in any part of the market may be sufficient. If, for example, it is confidently expected on the basis of past research and experience in the market that reaction to a new promotion will be highly correlated with the existing levels of sales per family, then there is a basis for projection and results from one area may be projectable on to other areas.

The converse will apply where regional differences are expected to operate, but where little can be forecast about their pattern or about the factors with which they are related. In these cases, it is unwise, to say the least, to take major decisions only on the basis of results from a single experimental area. Experiments in at least two areas, and preferably more, are essential if a reasonable assessment is to be made of the likely results of introducing the project into a wider area.

This situation will often lead to a clash between the scale acceptable on the grounds of budgets or pull-out costs and that required to give the necessary degree of precision in the results. A policy decision must then be made, either to change the nature of the experiment or else to accept a higher budget or a higher limit on pull-out costs or a higher degree of uncertainty in the results.

Such a situation would, for example, arise if a new product was to be test launched in Great Britain with television advertising available only in the pattern of area transmissions set by the VHF stations and with a budget or maximum pull-out cost which limited the test to about 5 per cent of the population. In such circumstances it would be difficult to provide a test to cover more than a single television area, or which would adequately reflect wide regional variations. If a company in this situation still wishes to test-launch its product, either it must substitute press or some other form of advertising for television, so as to be able to use smaller areas for testing, or else it must accept a higher budget or pull-out cost; or it must accept that the results may give only a poor indication of expectations in the wider market.

A compromise solution

An interesting set of conditions arises when a new project has a high expectation of success in itself, but where there is considerable uncertainty about the level of activity which may develop. If planning at too high a level would lead to losses, while planning at too low a level would lead to loss of potential profits, the argument in Chapter 3 would lead to a decision to test. This, however, can now be seen to lead to a sacrifice of profits in the area not covered by the test for as long as testing delays the wider launch. Again, two situations need to be recognized: first, where the bulk of the costs of launching are related to the level of activity or the volume of sales, and secondly where the larger part of the costs is dependent on the size of the marketing area. The first situation will arise where a major part of the costs come from investment in plant or production facilities; the second where the major element stems from advertising and marketing costs.

Where costs are more strongly linked to volume it becomes useful to consider the possibility of setting up facilities for producing at one of the lower possible levels, where there is a high expectation that sales of at least this chosen level will be made on the wider market. This will be below other levels which the company has some reasonable expectation of selling, but which also carry some risk of failure, and which, if planned for and not achieved, would result in losses. The product of the facilities established on the lower planning level would then be marketed experimentally in that fraction of the total market in which they could meet such of the higher potential levels of demand as can reasonably be expected and in the assurance that if demand reaches those levels it can be met.

One company was fully confident that it could sell over £200,000 worth of a new product profitably if planning was at the correct level. The most likely level was expected to be £500,000 with an expectation of 30 per cent, but the costs were such that a commitment on this basis would become unprofitable if sales failed to rise above £400,000. The mechanics of the situation were such that a smaller plant could be extended, but any reduction in the size of a plant already built would yield little more than scrap value.

In these circumstances the initial construction of a plant able to meet demand at £200,000, and the launch of the product into about 40 per cent of the market, provided a compromise avoiding the risks of heavy losses, while the test area was extended to the maximum to reduce the sacrifice of profits. Measurements in this area indicated a national market worth about £400,000, and the plant and marketing area were subsequently extended profitably.

Where a major part of the cost is linked to the area of the market covered, as would be the case if the costs were largely in the advertising or marketing areas, the problem becomes one of the type discussed earlier, of balancing costs and risks to determine the size of the experimental area smaller than the whole market.

6

Designing marketing experiments

The problems of how to design experiments have been the subject of a great deal of study by statisticians, who have sought to devise the most efficient ways of obtaining results with the minimum expenditure of resources. Some very elegant designs have been developed, and these have greatly improved experimental work in the physical sciences as well as in such areas as agriculture, botany, and biology.

Similar designs can sometimes be used in the pre-testing stages of product development, pack design, and other components of the marketing mix, where individual respondents can be subjected to such prescribed 'treatments' as being given specified alternative flavours for comparison. Then the use of more sophisticated statistical designs for experiments can greatly improve their efficiency, either by providing more precise results from a given sample of people or by enabling a given degree of accuracy to be achieved with smaller samples of contacts.

In experiments conducted in the market-place itself, the scope for using these more powerful but more complex designs is generally limited to small-scale experiments, like those in which experimental point-of-sale material is first exposed in a number of stores. In the more usual forms of marketing experiments involving wider areas and mass media, there is little scope for these more complex designs once the various constraints imposed by the size of the areas, the resources available, the size of the sales force, or the sheer nature of marketing itself have been taken into account. Often the only freedom left in the design of the experiment is a choice between two or three possible areas, of which only one can be afforded in any case.

Most marketing experiments then tend to be simple in design through force of circumstance, but despite this, or perhaps because of it, every opportunity should be taken to ensure that, whatever design is used, however simple it may be and however stringent the constraints imposed by other factors, it is as scientific as it is possible to make it.

Objectives of experimental design

In an ideal situation – unfortunately uncommon in marketing – the design used in an experiment should enable data to be collected and analysed so as to provide:

1 Measurements of changes or movements generated by the project.
2 A basis for assessing the reliability of the results.
3 A basis for projecting the results from the experimental situation to the wider market in terms sufficiently precise to meet the objectives of the experiment.

Consider first the problems of merely describing the present state of the market within which the experiment is to take place, and suppose that the experiment is concerned with action to change some factor among the population measurable through a normal consumer survey, e.g. awareness, attitudes, usage, etc. Such a survey would be designed not merely to provide national data under the appropriate headings, but also data for different geographic regions, class groups, age groups, and so on, so that these differences could be studied and understood. In the British context this is likely to involve contacting at least 2,000 people, and frequently more, depending largely on the number of geographic areas to be analysed separately and the nature of the market.

Regional differences

In most marketing situations there will be regional differences in the results obtained, arising from differences in population characteristics, the physical environment, or the different marketing histories of the products involved. Whatever the cause, the objective of an experiment, and particularly of a projectable experiment, is to enable assessments to be made of the impact of the proposed change in each of these areas on the basis of observations of its effects when it is introduced into only a few, or even only one, of the areas. This regional or area aspect of the projection situation is often lost sight of when national projections are made, but it is basically what is being attempted in any projectable test operation. The direct application of experimental results to the mean situation in a national market is essentially a short-cut method, and the use of the longer method of building up the national figures by aggregating area data will, by leading to a deeper understanding of the projection, generally reduce the risks of taking wrong decisions. This topic will be dealt with in more detail in Chapters 7 and 10.

Regional differences are of direct concern in the design of experiments, and even though the full rigour of statistical design theory can seldom be applied to market experiments, an understanding of the basic principles will help to avoid some of the pitfalls as well as in appreciating some of the limitations imposed on practical experiments.

Variation within and between areas

Suppose that over a whole country half the people in a market – whether involving housewives, men, all adults, or whatever – use a particular product, 'usage' being suitably defined. Clearly there will be variation of usage between people, some using the product and some not. Analysis by areas on a suitable basis may show that this 50 per cent level of usage holds over all areas, i.e. that there is no variation between areas

Figure 6.1

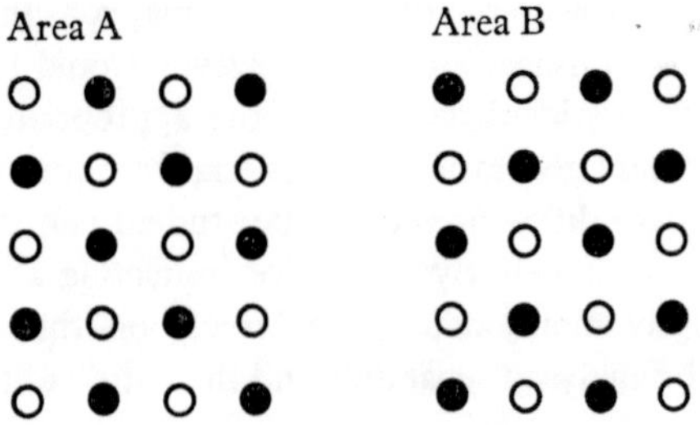

Area A   Area B

High variation within areas, but none between areas

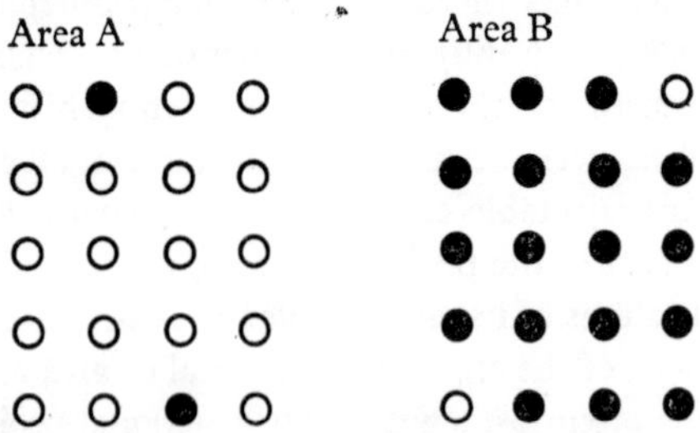

Area A   Area B

High variation between areas, but little within areas

in the proportions using, while within each area there will still be variation between individuals, half using the product and half not. This is an extreme case, where the whole variation among the population is confined within areas, none of it operating to give any variation between areas.

A different position would be shown in this analysis by areas if the national average of 50 per cent usage was the result of usage being

10 per cent in some areas and 90 per cent in the remainder. Here there would be less variation between the individuals within any single area – the people would be more alike than in the 50–50 split – but there would be a marked degree of variation between the different areas.

Basically, the greater the variation between areas, the larger the number of them which will need to be incorporated into an experimental design if the national pattern is to be projected with the required degree of accuracy. If it is known that there is no variation between areas, and all are expected to react to an equal, although unknown, extent, then measurements made in any one area will be typical of all, and no additional information is gained if the number of areas in the experiment is increased. If there is marked variation between areas, or markedly different reactions are expected to the experiment, no single area is capable of providing information to describe the remainder and each additional area included in the design provides additional information, although with decreasing marginal utility.

The variation between units within areas is an indication of the effort required to secure measurements of the state of the market in an area with any given degree of precision. In the unlikely event of all units within any area being identical, leading to no variation within areas, a sample of one unit will describe the entire area population. Usually there is some degree of variation, and the greater it is the more units must be sampled, – whether they be stores, homes, or individuals – if the required degree of precision in the results is to be gained.

Given that certain resources are available for an experiment, knowledge or forecasts of the magnitudes of the between-area and within-area variances can be used to calculate the optimum balance between numbers of areas and the numbers sampled within each to gain maximum precision in the results. Conversely, the calculations can indicate the optimum balance necessary if a specified degree of accuracy in the results is to be achieved with minimum expenditure on research. Unfortunately, the freedom of manoeuvre needed to take advantage of this situation is generally limited to laboratory conditions, and is normally lacking in marketing experiments, owing to the practical or political constraints imposed. Consequently there is little point in proceeding to a detailed discussion of such methods. There is, however, some point in discussing the broad implications so that certain risks inherent in most marketing experiments can be identified and in the hope that, wherever possible, certain basic principles may be more widely applied.

Assessment of area variations

The first principle is that some formal assessment of area variations in the product field concerned should be made as early as possible in the development of any experimental programme that is designed to yield projectable results. Where the experiments are concerned with an existing product, the material for the assessment will probably already exist in various research reports. Where a new product is to be test launched into a market not previously covered by the company, reasonable foresight should lead to the data being assembled during he later stages of product development or pre-testing, although it is still not uncommon for companies to enter the test-launch stage woefully ignorant on this subject. Without such knowledge, an experimental design may well fail to achieve even the limited efficiency possible within the constraints imposed by other factors; no proper appreciation of the risks involved will be possible, and the results may therefore be invested with an unwarranted aura of precision, while the resulting projections may be widely misleading.

Replication

The second principle is that the experiment should be launched in more than one area, and generally in as many as possible in the light of other factors. This is known statistically as replication.

In the majority of marketing experiments, this is more likely to be regarded as a pious hope than as a principle, because there may be little or no opportunity for using more than a single area. It should, however, be realized that in such cases a principle of good statistical design is being sacrificed, and that as a result certain risks and penalties are being accepted. The main risk is that unexpected area differences may develop during the experiment that will remain undetected because no comparisons can be made between areas. The main penalty is that certain statistical methods of assessing the effects of area variations on the precision of the final results cannot be applied to single-area data.

The smaller the extent of variation that exists between areas, the fewer areas will be needed for optimal experimental design; or, conversely, the smaller the variation that exists between areas, the more the confidence that can be attached to the results of an experiment necessarily limited to a small number of areas, or even to single area tests. In the examples used above, the situation where there is no variation between areas could normally be adequately covered by a two-area test, and although a single-area test should still be avoided if at all possible, the results will generally be acceptable. In the other case, however, where there is marked variation between areas, the absolute minimum to provide any sort of 'representation' of the market is two areas, and any single-area test would involve grave risks. In practical marketing conditions, where variation between areas is more likely to occur as a scattering of area means about the national level and not as the neat split into two levels which we are using here for illustration, more than two areas will be needed to provide a solid design and to minimize the risk of misleading results.

A further factor needs to be considered at this stage: that is, the nature of the experimental change itself. There is always a risk that even a market not showing any marked variations between areas may well contain some factors which vary regionally and which will become operative during the course of the experiment. For example, if a humorous or cartoon campaign is to be used for a product for which this is a marked departure from previous policy, regional differences in response may begin to operate for the first time where they would not have affected a new campaign along established lines. Similarly, while a 'me-too' product may not generate new regional differences, it would be unwise to assume that this would be true of a revolutionary product introduced on an experimental launch. For these reasons it is invariably safer to conduct an experiment in at least two areas – even where little regional difference exists – in case the subject of the experiment itself generates such differences.

Where area differences already exist in a market, there is an additional risk that the response to the experiment may in some way be linked to these differences. An area in which usage is above average may show little response in an experiment if saturation has already been reached there. Alternatively, however, the existing high level might be a reflection of above average potential which could be tapped by the experiment and so lead to a higher level of change than could be reproduced in other areas.

It is sometimes argued that such considerations do not apply in experimental launches of new products, because the new product has no share of the market anywhere; but this is a fallacy. Where an existing pattern of brand shares is uniform, then the penetration of the new product may be uniform, but where prior differences exist between areas, and where the new product may gain share differentially from the existing brands because of different prices, flavours, perfumes, etc., then the ultimate performance of the new product may be closely linked to the pattern in the area prior to the launch. Thus different areas may throw up different results, and single-area testing will be unreliable.

The only way in which proper diagnoses of differential experimental results can be made is through a comparison of results from a number of areas under different initial sets of conditions. In a paper in *Commentary*, Appel* gives an example where the response to experimental promotions depended on the level of penetration of the product prior to the experiment, and it was only because the experiment covered a number of areas that this effect could be determined and taken into account in assessing the results. In this particular case, two alternative promotions were being tested, and if only a single area had been used for each of them, the alternative which by chance was put into the area with the higher existing penetration of the product would probably have achieved the more favourable result, irrespective of its relative merit.

The risks of single-area tests

Clearly the validity of any assumptions that the risk of differential regional reactions can be ignored, and that a single-area test can be safely undertaken, must be examined very carefully in each instance. On a statistical basis, the single area is unsound; in practice, it is often the only option open to a company, and either it must be accepted or the experiment abandoned. Such acceptance should, however, only be made with a full realization of the dangers and limitations inherent in the situation.

The statistical unsoundness of experiments in which the proposed change is exposed in a single area is not only because the single area chosen may be in some way atypical, but also because the 'design' of such an experiment will prevent any assessment of area variations in response being measured and used to assess the precision of the results. When two or more sets of results are available from different areas, then an assessment can be made of the degree of variability that may be expected in the remaining areas of the wider market not yet involved. Where the variations between areas are narrow, there can be more confidence in the projections; where the variations are wide, then projections can only be made with less confidence.

Theoretically, calculations can be made of the variance of the results which will enable precise limits to be set to the projections and lead to statements of results in the form of the observed or projected results $\pm$ a range of error, e.g. a market share of 15 ± 3 per cent. The validity of such calculations strictly rests on certain conditions being observed in the design of the experiment that can seldom be applied in marketing situations – such as the selection of the test areas at random from the

* See Further Reading, page 183.

whole set of areas in the market. Where, as usually happens, constraints limit the areas suitable for the proposed experiment to only a few, often only two or three, of the total available, such calculations are not strictly valid and should only be used with considerable caution. This is particularly the case where experimental areas have been hand-picked for a special purpose, such as ensuring the inclusion of two widely separated geographical areas, or of an affluent area and one less fortunate where the resultant differences between areas may be artificially increased above the levels to be expected in random selection and so lead to estimates of the variance of the results above the true levels and unfavourable assessments of their precision.

Control areas

The third principle of experimental design is that arrangements should be made for a suitable 'control'. This means that measurements similar to those made in the experimental area will be made also in areas not subject to the experiment, for purposes of comparison. The necessity for this arises because there is always the possibility, greater in some markets than in others, but always present in some measure, that events will take place in the market generally while the experiment is in progress which, if not separately measured, could be mistaken for experimental effects. The purpose of the control is therefore to indicate what would have been expected to happen in the experimental area without the stimulus of the experiment, so that a proper assessment of the results can be made.

Where the experiment is concerned with an existing product, data from normal on-going research, from *ad hoc* surveys or panels of stores or consumers, will normally provide such control data anyway, and the experimental results will automatically be compared with progress in the rest of the market. The same situation applies in experimental launches where the product is in the same product field as others which the company is already marketing and covering by research. In these cases, the control data or its equivalent already exists independently of preparations for the experiment and no further effort or expenditure is needed.

In experimental launches of products in fields in which the companies concerned have not previously been engaged, the need for a valid control is easily ignored or overlooked. This failing is often rationalized by the fallacious reasoning that there is no point in making measurements in areas into which the new product has not yet been introduced. Yet there are few instances where a new product, however revolutionary, is launched into a vacuum where it does not have to compete for users who have previously bought existing products. Without a control, it must be assumed that any changes in sales or shares of existing products are due to the experimental launch, whereas they may in fact be due to other wider changes which merely affect the test area in common with the rest of the market. The same is true for measurements of the size of the total market in the area, where an observed increase in total sales may be credited to the experiment, but may merely be due to a warm summer or other changes in the environment which are affecting other areas simultaneously.

Apart from its use in assessing more specifically any changes resulting from an experiment, whether it is concerned with a new or an existing product, control data often has another useful function in that it enables the basic information for projection to be up-dated and possibly projected into the future before the effects of the experiment are applied to it. For example, suppose that, in accordance with our first principle, detailed research has been carried out on the market prior to the experiment, and that the experiment runs for nine months before an adequate result can be obtained. The application of the experimental results to the wider market situation as it was before the test started will then introduce an unnecessary additional error component into any national forecasts. The forecast will indicate what would have been expected to happen in the wider market had the innovation been introduced into it at the time when the experiment started, whereas what is required is a forecast of what may be expected to happen over the next nine months if the innovation is introduced into the wider market now. This latter forecast can only be made if the basic data on the state of the market can itself be currently up-dated, preferably with an assessment of trends within it so that forecasting has a dynamic and not a static basis. This depends on some measurement of the market having been made in a control area not affected by the test, and as will be seen in Chapter 10, preferably with measurements in each of the major areas in the remainder of the wider market.

In marketing experiments on a smaller scale than tests in which a change is put into an 'area', whether city, television area, or whatever, and promulgated through normal channels, controls are still needed if anything but the broadest inferences are to be read into the results. In some cases again, the results of current on-going research may be suitable where analyses of the data can be made to yield specific comparisons with the experimental situation. Thus, if samples or coupons are to be dropped in a limited number of streets with the object of studying subsequent purchasing patterns, comparable data from households outside the experiment may be obtainable from existing household panel research. When, however, the experiment is limited to a very specific part of the market, it is usually safer to set up a separate control, matching it so far as is possible to the experimental group. An experiment with a promotion specifically geared to stores belonging to a particular chain or voluntary group should be set up with a control drawn from other similar stores in the same organization, so as to avoid any risk that the organization as a whole is not already bucking the trends which may obtain in the market generally and which would be those thrown up by a normal store audit.

In such situations, and similar ones, as where households or streets may be used in sampling or couponing, the ideal method of proceeding is to select as many units (e.g. shops or streets) as may be required to provide both the experimental facility and the control, to stratify or arrange the units in groups according to their known characteristics, and then to allocate units within each stratum either to the experiment or to the control groups at random, so that it is purely a matter of chance which group they fall into. Opportunities for such closely controlled experiments are rare in marketing, and are usually limited to small-scale experiments of the type discussed here. The close control will often make it possible to use much more sophisticated experimental designs, followed by more penetrating analytical techniques such as analysis of variance in determining the true magnitude of the results. Discussion of these highly specialized procedures and techniques is however outside the scope of the present book.

Time in experimental design

The fourth principle is that sufficient time should be allowed for a valid experiment to be completed and measured. Time is a factor in experimental design, and it is needed for three specific purposes:

1 So as to obtain measurements of the state of the market in both experimental and control areas prior to the introduction of the innovation.
2 For the proper introduction of the experimental factor and the build-up of whatever effects may be produced.
3 Further time is then needed to observe longer-term movements after the initial impact.

Where existing research can provide back-data on the experimental and control areas to be used, the time required to obtain initial measurements of the state of the market becomes of no importance, but where research facilities have to be set up from scratch, or where, although there may be existing facilities, measurements have not previously been made in the product field involved, some specific time must be allowed for. Apart from any time needed to establish panels or other research media, time must be allowed for at least one reporting period, and preferably more, prior to the experiment. If the measurements are to be made, for instance, on a four-weekly or two-monthly basis, these periods must be allowed for. While it can be possible to telescope the timing by collecting and analysing data over shorter base periods of, say, two weeks or one month, thus establishing a rate for the longer periods, this again introduces some uncertainty into the system as to the validity of any subsequent comparisons. True, this may be only a slight additional measure of uncertainty, but the whole object of designing efficient experiments is to keep uncertainty to a minimum, and even small potential increments should be avoided.

Where a run of base data is available, from existing sources or through an ability to set up research facilities well ahead of the experiment's introduction, there may be additional benefits at the analysis stage from an opportunity to compare not only averages or mean levels before and after the experiment, but also to examine the period to period variations in the results through an analysis of variance. Where such data is likely to be available in an experiment, statistical help should be sought in order to take full advantage of any opportunities for deeper analysis.

The second time-consuming phase is during the introduction of the experimental factors and the build-up of their effects. Generally, if projections are to be made from the results with any reasonable degree of precision, these factors must be allowed to develop at their natural rates; attempts to speed-up the processes or to 'hot-house' the experiment should be avoided. Where, however, precise projection is not the major objective, but less specific indicators of the effects are being sought, then it may be justifiable to use 'hot-housing' through such means as running a campaign at increased frequency for a shorter period; by using commando salesmen to obtain distribution more rapidly; by inducing more rapid repurchase in the field to test repeat buying; or by other means. Inevitably, however, such methods again introduce new elements of uncertainty into the situation, raising such questions as whether the concentration of a campaign may make it more effective anyway, whether more rapid distribution may give added impetus to a launch, or whether speeding up the buying cycle may not affect the brand bought. For these reasons, the problem of projecting the results will become more difficult, and new sources of bias may be introduced whose direction and magnitude may be unpredictable.

The third phase is needed to provide time for the effects to stabilize, and to avoid the risks of taking as final observed levels of achievement which are only transient. With experimental launches (or, indeed, wider launches) of new products, sales will normally build up to a peak and then decline to a stable level, the whole process taking up to a year or more. Since there are as yet no means of forecasting for any one product how far sales will drop from the peak to the stable level – the average

Figure 6.2

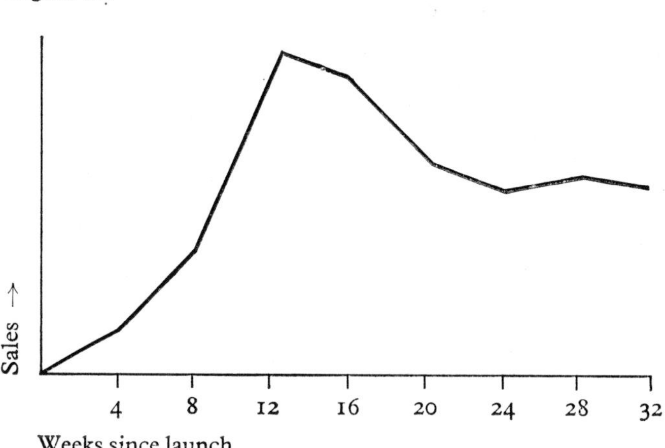

drop appears to be about 40 per cent, but the range of results observed is virtually from 0 per cent to 100 per cent – it is highly dangerous to take action on any experimental readings until it is quite clear that stability has been reached, however high the initial sales levels may go in comparison with any targets. Premature termination of an experimental launch will almost certainly lead to optimistic assessments of results. While no specific timings can be laid down, study of previous launches in the product field should provide at least some indication of the minimum time likely to be necessary to achieve stability. Failing this, general experience suggests that fast-moving packaged goods may take between six months and a year to settle down, and effective assessments of the results must depend on a time-span of this order. For slower moving products, with longer repurchase cycles, the time needed to achieve stability will normally be greater, and at least six times the average repurchase cycle should be regarded as a minimum· Conversely, there are a few products where the repurchase cycle is measured in hours or days and where other favourable factors lead to a rapid build-up of initial trial, and in these cases stability may be achieved more quickly.

With experiments in marketing existing products, the same considerations apply, and time must be allowed for any initial benefits to stabilize. Where the experiment is concerned with assessing the effects of such changes as a reduction in an appropriation or an increase in price or the substitution of ingredients, i.e. where, if there is any movement, a fall in sales may be expected, then it may be several months before any change is observed at all. A number of experiments of this nature have probably been abandoned too quickly because no measurable results have been observed after, say, six months. Had the experiment mentioned in Chapter 4 (page 63) been terminated after six, nine, or even twelve months, this could have amounted to a disastrous decision.

As a corollary to any discussion on timing, it is always worth considering the possibility of maintaining measurements in experimental areas after the initial purposes of the tests have been satisfied, if the project is to be adopted on a wider scale. A means is then available for experimenting with any subsequent developments under conditions already a year or so ahead of the main market, and at a stage of development likely to be similar to that which may be expected to obtain in the wider market if, and when, this next development is introduced there.

Complex designs

The discussion so far applies to all forms of marketing experiments, but certain additional factors are involved where the experiments cease to be simple tests to assess whether some single innovation or change will be effective in reaching a particular goal and become concerned with assessing which of two or more possible courses of action will be most beneficial. A product may be launched experimentally in two or more forms, or with different prices or campaigns. Experiments on advertising pressure may cover a range of alternatives, or those involving couponing may cover a range of values. Various campaigns may be available, rather than a single alternative, or assessments may be needed to show the relative merits of above or below the line expenditure, or expenditure in different media, or in different types of promotional activity. In certain more sophisticated experimental programmes, the objective is not merely to assess which of several specified levels of activity will be most beneficial, but also to determine the optimum level of activity or combination of activity levels.

Where a single factor is being used experimentally – such as price, or advertising pressure, or the campaign, or promotions, or whatever – an extension of the experiment to cover a number of alternatives calls for the provision of at least as many experimental areas as there are treatments, and preferably more. It may occasionally, and after careful consideration, be possible to run experiments in sequence, with one alternative after another being applied within the same experimental area, but this is rare. Apart from the long time-span needed for sequential experiments, once an area has been used for testing at one level it is no longer on the same footing as the remainder of the main market, and reactions to any subsequent changes may be seriously affected.

Consider, for example, a case where price increases of 5, 10, and 15 per cent are being tested to determine which would be most profitable. Introduced into a single area in sequence, there can be no guarantee that the levels of sales observed as the price is increased from 105 to 110 per cent, and then to 115 per cent, will reflect the levels which would result from direct increases to the higher levels. The reverse procedure of testing the 115 per cent level first, followed by 110 and 105 per cent, is clearly unlikely to produce valid results. Similar considerations normally apply to steps in a pressure test, or series of different campaigns, etc., and reliable results can only be obtained from the use of separate areas.

Even in situations where testing in sequence may be feasible, a further complication arises because each alternative will be tested during a different time-span and 'all other things' in marketing conditions may not remain equal, thus introducing a further source of error into the results.

Increasing the effectiveness of experiments

One problem common to all forms of experimentation, but more acute where comparisons are to be made between alternative treatments, is that the differences generated may be comparatively small, but still of major importance. In a market where total sales are £10m a year, a change in brand share of 1 per cent is worth £100,000 in sales, but to design an experiment capable of detecting such a change and of differentiating it from ordinary market fluctuations will normally call for far more than the one or two areas generally available. It will also call for a degree of precision in the measurements made within each area that is generally beyond the competence of the samples of about 100 food stores or a few hundred households which tend to be used in many experiments.

There are a number of ways in which some contribution can be made to solving the problem, apart from the obvious but expensive statistical solutions of increasing the number of areas and increasing the sizes of the samples used within them.

One method is virtually a form of 'hot-housing', but it is used with the object of producing a more measurable exaggerated result rather than merely trying to speed the completion of the experiment. One field in which this can be contemplated is in the pressure testing of advertising. Situations arise here where it may be believed that there is considerable scope for increasing sales through an increased investment in advertising, but, for various reasons, such as immediate cash-flow, only a modest increase can be considered and this is put forward for testing. The increase in sales expected or hoped for is, again, only modest, and would be difficult, if not impossible, to detect with the available research. One possibility here, then, is to gear the test to a far higher increase in media expenditure in the test area, sufficiently large, if expectations are realized, for a clear movement in sales to be achieved and measured. The results are then used to interpolate the movement which might be expected if only the lower level of increase could be applied to the market, usually on the reasonable assumption that the relationship between advertising and sales in the relatively limited interval between existing and experimental levels of expenditure will be linear.

Another way of squeezing the last ounce of information out of an experiment – and this is, after all, the essence of experimental design – is the cross-over design. This consists of running the experiment initially in the experimental areas against suitable control areas. Once a result has been observed, the experimental factor is introduced into the control areas to assess whether the original results can also be observed there. Confirmation of both the magnitude and the timing of effects will, of course, greatly increase the confidence which can be placed in the results, however small their magnitude.

Any experimental situation can present opportunities for obtaining increased efficiency through variations in design. Each situation needs to be assessed on its merits, in the light of the factors involved and of the constraints which may be imposed, so as to arrive at the design which makes optimum use of the available resources. This is the province of the statistician, and if one is available, either from within the company or from outside, he should be brought into the discussion at an early stage. He may at first find himself horrified at the context within which he has to work, particularly if his background experience has been with laboratory or industrial experiments, but he will almost certainly be able to make a valuable contribution.

7

Selection of experimental areas

The inclusion of this chapter is an admission that experiments in marketing are generally unscientific, and this is because of the constraints imposed upon them.

In scientific experiments in the laboratory, or in field trials in agriculture or horticulture, experiments are carried out a number of times or simultaneously over a number of different subjects or plots. The results are treated as 'samples' out of the whole universe of results which could be obtained if the experiment was repeated an infinite number of times, and the validity of the final conclusions rests on these samples being 'representative' and sufficient in number to provide the required degree of precision. To avoid bias, and to provide results which are representative, the whole process of selecting apparatus, subjects, plots, or whatever, is carried out in ways that ensure that the final allocation depends on chance alone, and that no bias, human or otherwise, can creep in. Then it becomes possible to analyse the results on the basis of the known laws of probability, and to be confident that a 'representative' result has been obtained within calculable limits of precision.

Some areas of market research do allow similar operations to be undertaken, as, for example, in a well-financed and well-conducted consumer survey where random selection of the individuals to be interviewed is used. This will mean that, within the defined population, it is a matter of chance and chance alone as to which individuals are included and which are not, and the results can be accepted as representative within limits of error that can be calculated from the data itself. (In some cases, bias may creep in from refusals or non-contacts, or from other sources, but the principle of unbiased itiinal selection stands.)

In the conditions applying to scientific experiments or surveys among the population, the problems of selection are all concerned with organizing unbiased samples of measurements that will then be representative of all the measurements that might have been made. The processes are carried out in ways which remove selection completely from the hands, or the mind, of the researcher.

Constraints in marketing experiments

In marketing experiments, the process of selecting the areas to be used is usually completely different. Normally, the number of areas permitted for reasons of budget, administration, or availability of facilities is limited, sometimes to ten or twelve, but more usually to only one or two. Given an opportunity to use only one or two areas, marketing men are wisely reluctant to allow the selection to depend on chance, because under such limiting conditions there would only be a small 'probability' of obtaining a representative sample of areas and so the limits of error would be too wide, if calculable at all, for the results to be of practical value. Hence, chance selection is generally abandoned, even if it is ever considered, and a search is begun for 'typical' areas. Scientific methods are abandoned because under the conditions imposed they cannot be properly applied, and human judgement has to be substituted.

Before considering the criteria that may be applied in assessing the typicality of a potential experimental area, two other sets of criteria need to be considered that may filter out some at least of the areas potentially available. These are criteria concerned with the amenability of an area to the conditions of the experiment, and the measurability of results of the required type. Both these sets of criteria are commonly taken into account, although often on a somewhat vague basis.

Amenability

For an area to be amenable to an experiment, it must naturally possess the basic facilities required. These may be such media facilities as press, television, radio, or outdoor advertising; distribution facilities, either general or specific, such as a company depot or wholesale or retail outlets of particular types; or, in some cases, other specific attributes such as docks, light engineering, sea-bathing, winter snow, or whatever may be required to provide an effective environment for the experiment. These considerations will lead to the definition and listing of the areas potentially available for the experiment within the constraints set by problems of budgeting or administration.

Measurability

The problems of measurability depend on what is to be measured and how it is to be done, and both of these may affect the choice of area. In some circumstances there may be a need for areas to be separated so far as possible from neighbouring areas, but in others it may be possible to use an area deeply embedded in a conurbation without imposing any handicap. This will depend on how far movements of goods or people across the area boundaries may affect the measurements made. If depot sales are the only measure that can be afforded, then areas must be selected not only where these can be analysed separately, but also where the analysis is closely related to a definite marketing area – which will mean using areas naturally cut off in some way from their neighbours so as to minimize the flow to areas outside the experiment. If store audits are to be used to assess the effects of in-store promotions, isolation ceases to be a factor, at least so far as measurement is concerned. If, however, store audits are being used to measure the effects on sales of changes in advertising, movement of people into the area from outside the reach of the local media could dilute any effects and

Figure 7.1 Penetration of two overlapping media

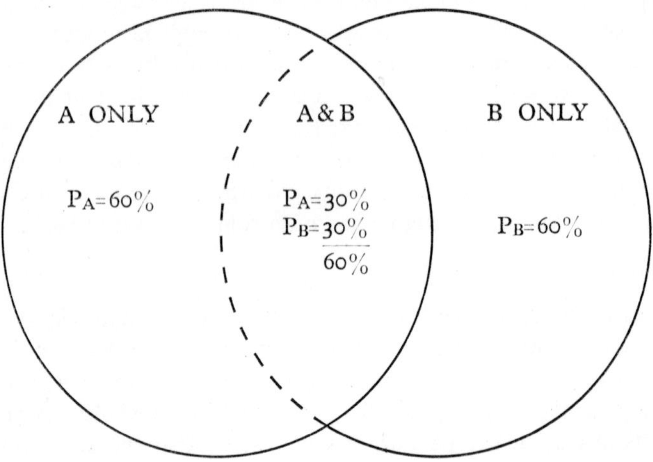

lead to biased results, and here isolation would be an advantage. Yet again, however, if measurements were to be made through a consumer panel whose members could be located within the reach of the media, isolation would cease to be a factor and true measurements of the effects could be obtained irrespective of where the panel members shopped or who came into the area from outside to shop.

It is worth emphasizing that there need not necessarily be any close correspondence between the area covered by the factors involved in an experiment and the area in which measurements are to be made. The area of measurement can be, and often should be, smaller than the area reached by the factors, whether in an experimental launch or in other forms of market testing. This is owing to the problems created by overlapping media facilities, and it can be illustrated by considering a simplified case involving only two facilities, say two local newspapers, A and B (see Figure 7.1).

An experimental campaign is to be run in area A to decide whether it should be introduced into the wider market covered by both areas together. The penetration of A in its solus area is 60 per cent, and of B in its solus area 60 per cent, and in the overlap area which accounts for one third of the population in the circulation area of A, 30 per cent of people read A and 30 per cent B.

If some kind of measurements, whether of sales, attitudes, opinions, or whatever, are now made in the whole circulation area covered by A, they will have been influenced by an effective rate of penetration of the medium not of 60 per cent, but only of 50 per cent, this being the average of 60 per cent penetration over two thirds of the population and 30 per cent over the remaining third. If the campaign is ultimately run in both media A and B, the effective penetration will be 60 per cent everywhere and the experimental measurements are being made under less favourable conditions than would then be available. The situation can, of course, be remedied by restricting the measurements to the area covered by A which does not overlap with B, when the required condition of 60 per cent penetration will prevail. This is the reason why many of the permanent test panels operated by media owners are more limited than the full area they cover; in this way dilution through overlap areas, or through the frequent attenuation in penetration which occurs as distance from source increases, is avoided.

In assessing potential experimental areas for measurability, these problems of defining the boundaries need careful consideration in the light of the experiment's objectives. Generally experiments call for an assessment of effects produced when a market is subjected to a particular 'weight' of stimulus, and measurements should therefore be made only within the area where this is achieved. The fact that achieving the required conditions within an experimental area means that other areas receive the same stimulus, but under conditions not according with the experiment, is incidental and should not be allowed to cloud the issue.

It follows from this discussion that the problems involved in selecting areas and the problems of measurement are closely interlinked. In some circumstances the selection of particular areas will dictate whatever methods of measurement will have to be used to obtain valid results; in others the decision to use particular methods of measurement may lead to some potential areas being rejected as the results could not be properly measurable by those methods in these instances.

Typicality

The third set of criteria is concerned with the search for typicality, or, to be more precise, with detecting and excluding the more atypical areas since no area can ever be typical of a larger market in more than a few respects. Areas in the north of a country are generally woefully short of southerners or vice versa, and even where there are no actual measurable ethnic differences, there may be differences in speech, customs, humour, and attitudes to change which can all be important within the context of an experiment.

Routine examination of potential areas for atypicality starts with census reports or other sources of demographic data, and is concerned with the composition of the area population in terms of sex, age, terminal age of education, socio-economic or occupational characteristics, and so forth. The smaller the types of area being considered, the wider the variations from national averages likely to be encountered. In Great Britain, towns of between 100,000 and 250,000 people will, as a group, show far more variation from the national averages than television areas will, and many will be rejected as being too atypical for use in a particular experiment. However, as there are far more such towns than there are television areas suitable for experimental use at the time of writing (1970), the use of towns still offers a wider choice of location in most cases.

Statistical techniques known as taxonomic analysis – developed originally in the fields of botany and biology to classify specimens of plants and animals – have been used to divide the collection of towns within a required range (say, between 100,000 and 250,000 inhabitants) into groups on the basis of demographic or other data, so that each town within a group is more like the others in that group than it is like any towns belonging to other groups. There can, of course, be considerable differences between different listings, depending on which characteristics are included in the analysis, the importance given to each, and the number of groups into which the whole list is divided. This is, however, merely an indication that this form of analysis is adaptable for various purposes, and any listings used should be based on a selection of attributes of some relevance to the particular experiment or market.

Taxonomic listings can be useful in three ways: (a) where only one or two towns are to be used, they will quickly indicate which towns fall into groups far removed from the national or other averages being used as criteria and so lead to their speedy elimination; (b) where control towns are to be used, they indicate those towns which have basically similar characteristics and enable experimental and control areas to be drawn from within a single group; (c) where the experiment will involve the use of a number of towns, they can, if homogeneity is required, be drawn from within a single group or else spread between groups if this would be advantageous. If the experiment is concerned with assessing which one from among alternative methods will give the more beneficial result, and each method is to be used in one town, the closer the similarity between the towns the better. On the other hand, if the object of the experiment is to assess the likely effects of introducing one specific option on a wider level by using a projectable test, it will generally be more beneficial to arrange that the towns used should cover a wide range of conditions and come from different groups in the list.

Area market patterns

After this general examination of potential areas, which will be similar for most markets, it is necessary to consider the market situation itself within each area, since there can be wide and important variations. The histories of brand development, the calibre of past and present personnel, any previous use of the area for testing, the relative importance of different wholesale or retail systems or organizations besides different consumer customs or attitudes can all lead to conditions in local areas being atypical in comparison with wider patterns.

At this level there may or may not exist a single norm – such as the national pattern – which can be accepted as a standard. As was seen in Chapter 5, it is quite possible for national figures to be merely the average of two or more types of area, but for no single area to show any similarity with these averages. The minimum requirement for any semblance of typicality is, under these conditions, the selection of as many experimental areas as there are major types of region in the whole market, and it may well be unsound to proceed on any other basis. Even where some potential areas do show the overall market pattern, it may be unwise to use them alone if variations in local patterns are extreme. For example, if the brand shares in a market are linked in some way with the hardness of the water and there are marked differences between hard and soft water areas, it may be possible to locate areas where the water is of average hardness that will show the national pattern of brand shares. It would, however, be dangerous to use average areas alone in the experimental launch of a revolutionary new product since there could be no guarantee that results there would represent the average of results obtainable in hard and soft water areas. Generally in such situations, if the pattern of area differences is such that most of the country conforms to the national pattern, then test areas which conform can be considered generally typical of most other areas. Where, however, less than half of the market is in this central group, and where there are large areas which do not conform to any average, it cannot be too strongly recommended that any search for one central aspect of typicality should be abandoned, and that the experiment should be mounted with at least one area to typify each of the major groups.

When smaller types of area are used it is unlikely that research data on the specific area market will be available in detail from existing services. In Great Britain, the syndicated services, whether based on store audits, consumer panels, or continuous questionnaire surveys, cannot normally provide market information for the smaller television areas, the local press circulation areas, or for individual towns. In some cases, where the media owners are supporting research facilities, the necessary information may be available and inquiries should certainly be made. Analyses of factory shipments of existing products may also be useful, but they need very careful consideration in most cases before any potential area can be either accepted or rejected on the strength of them. The mere presence or absence of a cash-and-carry wholesaler, or the head office of a local chain, may be sufficient to make deliveries into the area appear atypical, whereas sales to consumers within the area may not be affected.

In general, apart from certain inferences which may be drawn from available data, nothing very specific may be known about the market position within the potential list of areas, and it will usually be necessary to fall back on more subjective assessments based on existing knowledge of the areas or on information gathered during specific visits. This will generally be enough to indicate whether an area is widely atypical through the operation of certain local factors.

The more the suitability of an area for an experiment has to be taken on trust instead of being based on firm measurements of the market, the greater need there is for ample time for measurements to be taken prior to the actual start of the experiment. In the unlikely event that the area proves to be impossible, there may still be time to move to another location; but, more important, time should allow for the market to be properly measured and described before any of the effects of the experiment begin to appear. Where research facilities have to be set up specifically for an experiment, as opposed to using those that may already be maintained in an area by media or research companies, it is vital for the base period to be long enough to allow such facilities to settle down, and be seen to have settled down, before experimentation begins. There are few things more frustrating than being uncertain of the validity of experimental results because of doubts about the accuracy of base period figures.

Atypicality

Of the three factors amenability, measurability, and typicality, typicality is the least important. If an area is not amenable to the conditions of the experiment, no degree of measurability or typicality will remedy the situation, and an experiment there will be of little value. If the results of an experiment are not measurable in an area, the effort is worthless, even should the area be a perfect microcosm of the larger market. However, given amenability and measurability, some degree of atypicality can be accepted and allowed for in the interpretation of the findings, albeit with some potential loss in their accuracy. The problem is that one never knows precisely how much effect atypicality may have on the results; and no matter in how many respects an area may be found to be typical, it may still be atypical in other dimensions that have not been considered and which may have a marked effect on the results.

The ideal way round this dilemma is to mount experiments in a sufficient number of areas for it to be possible to use statistical methods to select a representative sample of them from all the areas available. This, at least within the foreseeable future, is a counsel of perfection, but when it becomes possible the advice given in this chapter can be ignored and chapters on sampling methods from statistical textbooks substituted.

8

Methods of measurement

There is no point in carrying out experimental work in any area unless proper provision is made for measuring the effects produced. Furthermore, the value of the experiment will probably be enhanced as the amount of data collected is increased and as measurements are collected at more points in the system.

Measurements made in experimental marketing may be used in a number of ways:

1 To provide the data on which decisions can be based, varying from the precise requirements for taking decisions in projectable test launching, campaign tests, pressure tests, etc., to the less rigorous needs of feasibility testing.
2 To provide information about the performance of the various parts of the marketing mix, and to indicate weaknesses or failures.
3 To provide a set of guidelines for any subsequent extension of the experimental situation into wider areas of the market.

Some measurements will provide information useful in all three ways, while most types of data will be useful in at least two of them. Thus knowledge of rates of consumer purchase will contribute to projections of national sales, show the ultimate effectiveness of the marketing mix, and automatically provide a norm with which to compare any subsequent efforts in a larger area. Knowledge of how awareness of a new product was built up during the initial period will not in itself contribute anything to a forecast of sales, but it will indicate how the advertising is performing and, again, provide a norm against which to compare subsequent results from a wider area.

In experiments involving most kinds of consumer goods, there are two main areas where measurements can be made. The first concerns the physical flow of the product from the manufacturer through wholesalers and warehouses to retail outlets and on to the consumers. This calls for sales analysis at the factory, and for the use of panels of wholesalers, or of retailers or consumers at the later stages of distribution.

The second area concerns the flow of information from the manufacturer to the consumer, with measurements being made at various points in time, ranging from the extent to which consumers are aware of the product at all to assessments of attitudes towards the product and the nature of its image. This type of measurement is carried out using appropriate sample surveys and questionnaire techniques.

Sales analysis

Sales analysis is concerned with the flow of goods out of the factory or warehouse, and most companies operate some system of sales analysis, whether or not they are experimenting. As with all forms of analysis, it should be organized to provide as much useful information as possible and ruthlessly trimmed from time to time to prevent the recurrent production of figures no longer of any value.

The use which can be made of sales analysis will vary from company to company and from product to product, and there is no one set of analyses to fit all circumstances. There are, however, certain forms of analysis which are generally useful and which tend to form the basis of most systems.

In most experimental situations, and certainly in experimental launches, it is useful to have a daily total count of orders received, goods dispatched, and stock in hand, with the first two cumulated into orders and dispatches to date. This will provide a picture of the way in which orders for the new product are building up, as well as giving early warning of any possible stock shortage. Even if nothing can be done to meet an out-of-stock situation, the fact that shortages occurred at all may be vital to any subsequent analysis or interpretation of results. Where established products are concerned, the normal analysis of sales on a monthly basis will usually be sufficient.

Since most manufacturers are dealing with a heterogeneous collection of direct customers, including, perhaps, wholesalers, co-operative societies, multiples, and individual shops in one dimension, as well as, perhaps, pharmacists, food stores, department stores, variety stores, etc., in another, it is generally useful to have sales to each major category analysed separately. From these analyses it is then possible to see not only where the goods are going, but also to assess, from the different ways in which the patterns develop, how the total market is likely to move. For example, when launching a new product, either as an experiment or in a wider area, it is not unusual for such larger customers as the multiples or co-operatives to be called on first, and daily orders from them may build up to a peak and begin to fall away again while orders from independent shops are still rising. Knowledge that this is happening will help to avoid the pitfall of assuming that when one quarter or one half of the canvass or cycle has been completed, the orders received can be multiplied by four or by two to get an estimate of total likely initial demand.

Sales analysis can be organized quite simply on the basis that every order delivered is related to a customer who is then coded to indicate the form of organization (wholesaler, co-operative, multiple, or independent retailer, etc.), the type of trade (pharmacist, food store, hardware, department store, etc.), the sales territory, television area, and any other relevant classification data useful to the manufacturer concerned.

With new products, the sales analysis system can be set up from scratch to provide whatever data is needed for the launch. When experimenting with existing products, one major factor that will determine how much use can be made of sales analysis will be the extent to which year-old data can be made available. Since it is usually easier to extract all analyses for a period at one time, rather than to reanalyse at a later point, it is frequently worth while to ensure that major analyses likely to be required for subsequent testing are produced when the figures are first processed. This could, for example, mean that some areas which might be used for experimental purposes, such as the circulation areas of selected local newspapers or some of the smaller television areas, would be separately analysed through time, even though there might be no immediate use for the results, so as to ensure that they will be readily available if required for experimental purposes. Even if this is not done as routine, it will still be valuable to ensure that the method of coding customers includes a sufficient geographic description to enable all customers in any small specified area to be identified and analysed at any time. This costs virtually nothing, whether the system is manual, mechanized, or computerized, and can be of great benefit when comparative analyses of back-data relating to a test area are needed. Thus a sound coding system will enable customers to be identified and analysed down to the small areas or single towns involved when using local newspapers, radio, or television.

The main breakdowns provided by sales analysis will normally be concerned with the shipments period by period – in quantity or value – to the various areas and types of customer. These can be handled in various ways, to show actual period by period totals, cumulative totals from the beginning of the financial year, or the season, or the launch of a new product, etc., and comparative figures such as percentage changes on last year or the previous period, the proportions of total sales going to each category, and so on can be produced. The need for these various types of data will be determined by the nature of the market, the way in which a company is organized, and the marketing objectives it is pursuing.

Clearly, when a product is being marketed in a number of sizes or flavours, or in other variations, analyses should take account of these and separate series of figures should be maintained for each one. It is not unusual for the ratios between variants to change considerably over time, and this can be particularly marked for new products where the initial trade orders may have been made on a somewhat arbitrary basis but where subsequent orders will more closely reflect consumer demand. Any shifts between variants observed in this way can quickly be compared with the marketing objectives and so serve as a basis for any appropriate action to encourage or resist the trend, and they can also, of course, be fed into production schedules and sales forecasts to prevent unnecessary shortages or stock-piling.

Apart from analyses of the movement of product in quantities or value, data should also be extracted – especially during test operations – to show the proportions of customers taking the product concerned and the degree of success being achieved in opening new outlets. Representatives' reports should also be checked for any observations relevant to the test, indicating any problems, difficulties, or successes which may have a bearing on the experiment's outcome.

As the experiment progresses, particularly if it is a launch, analyses of repeat orders become important, and although it may be laborious, some attempt should be made to keep a running record of the proportions of customers in the various categories who have ordered once, twice, three times, and so forth. For selected major customers, individual record cards of orders placed should be kept, or print-outs be made available, so that some early assessments can be made from the frequency of successive orders and their composition of the kind of acceptance the product is meeting.

Where a test takes place in a number of separated areas, then sales analysis will provide data for each separate cell. Where testing is taking place in larger areas, each containing a number of sales territories or journeys, then analyses should still be taken down to this level to show the extent of variations between territories and representatives. Such information is valuable in assessing the reliability of the results of test operations, but is also useful in providing warnings that, say, particular representatives may be meeting unusual difficulties, or else are so successful that they are possibly using unorthodox methods to secure orders, which could either be detrimental to the test or which should even be brought into general use if compatible with company policy.

The main thing about sales analysis is that it is usually inexpensive to carry out because the data required is already in the hands of the company in some form or other and has already been processed for invoicing purposes. Using the same data for sales analysis is then simply a matter of organization plus a small additional effort. The range of possible analyses is also such that, once an appropriate system has been thought out and applied, a large amount of valuable data becomes available for management, not only for test purposes but for normal purposes of control.

Wholesale and retail store audits

The progress of the product from the factory to the consumer can be measured at either wholesale or retail level by means of audit techniques. This is generally done only at retail level, and it is the retail store audit which will be described here, but the same techniques have been adapted to measuring flows of goods through wholesalers and multiple warehouses.

Since it is not normally economic for an individual manufacturer to recruit and train the necessary staff and to set up and operate a retail store audit, arrangements are usually made for a research company to carry out the work, either directly or, in some cases, through media proprietors operating in the area of the experiment.

The basic principles of retail auditing are simple, though their implementation is somewhat more complex. A panel of stores is selected to represent all stores of a particular description in a defined area, and arrangements are made with their respective owners or managers to visit them at regular intervals – usually every four weeks or every two months. At each visit stocks of the products being measured are counted and the quantities received since the previous visit are abstracted from invoices and delivery notes. From this data the following simple calculation can be made for each pack size of each brand being covered:

Stock at first call	a
Net deliveries since then	b
Total available for sale	$a + b$
Stock at second call	c
Sales during period	$a + b - c$

By adding together the values of each item obtained in each of the representative panel of stores, estimates can be made of the sales, stocks, etc., over all stores of that type in a given area. This information is collected through physical audits of stocks in the shops and trade documents and does not depend in any way on the memory or opinions of the retailer or his assistants. It does, however, call for meticulous stock counting for all the products covered, wherever they may be in the store or its stockrooms, and a very careful scrutiny of invoices and other documents, not all of which may be very clearly laid out or filled in. Hence the need for training and experience among research personnel working in the stores.

Retail audit panels provide data under four headings, and although the methods of presentation may vary from one research organization to another, these four basic sets of analyses will normally be provided for each pack size of each brand covered:

1 Distribution data will show the proportion of stores with the product actually in stock at the time of the audit and the proportion of stores which have handled it at any time since the previous audit. These results may be presented either as straight proportions of stores, or they may be weighted to show the proportion of total trade, through outlets of the type covered, which passes through the stores' stocking or handling. Thus a new product that has been taken up first by larger stores may be found in 40 per cent of all stores, but when weighted by turnover may be in stores responsible for 70 per cent of the total trade. Maximum value can, of course, be obtained from the research when both figures are given and can be compared.

2 Deliveries into the stores will be counted from invoices and delivery notes, etc., and will be shown by quantity and value. Results can either be shown in grossed-up terms to show estimated deliveries to all stores in the test area, or else in terms of the average deliveries per store. Either of these figures is, of course, easily convertible into the other, and any preference for one or the other will depend on the methods to be used in subsequent data manipulation. A third method of presentation is to calculate the average deliveries per store handling the product. This statistic depends, however, on both the volume of product and on its distribution, and is therefore not always easy to interpret and virtually useless for any further manipulation. A more useful variant in many cases is an analysis of deliveries according to their source – generally direct deliveries from the manufacturers as against deliveries from wholesalers or factors.

3 Consumer purchases or retailer sales will be shown in the same main ways as deliveries. These are usually the crucial figures in marketing experiments, on which the ultimate assessments will be made. The analysis of the sales per shop handling a new product can provide useful indications of likely development and should not be ignored.
4 Stocks in the retail stores will, again, be shown in the same general form as deliveries.

In addition to these basic series of data, other information can be collected at the time of the audit and other analyses be made available. Stock cover is often calculated, by dividing the level of stocks by the current level of consumer offtake, to indicate how long stocks in the stores would last at the current rate of purchase. Information can be collected on the extent of use of display material, or of showings or facings of the product, the prices being charged, and so forth. All this data, both the basic analyses and any supplementary analyses or data, can, of course, be made available for competitive products as well as the test product, and, where necessary, separate results can be provided for both normal packings and for any special promotions, deals, or offers. As the amount of detail provided is increased, the costs of obtaining the data will rise, and in some cases the size of the panel itself may need to be enlarged to ensure that the accuracy of some of the finer break-downs is not impaired. Thus, once the basic analyses have been covered, the costs of further detail must be balanced against the benefits they provide in the normal way.

Before an audit panel can be established, a decision is needed about the types of store it is to cover, the choice normally being between using panels of given types of stores or using panels of stores stocking particular product groups. In most countries today there are very few products which sell only through a single type of store, and most products will be found in several types. Frozen foods sell through fishmongers, butchers and greengrocers as well as grocers; car polishes sell through department stores, hardware stores, variety stores and supermarkets besides service stations; and cigarettes sell through a host of outlets besides tobacconists.

In some cases, distribution of a product group is so widespread among different types of store that the only effective audit panel will be one that will cover outlets for that product group irrespective of store type. Hence a comprehensive audit for cigarettes would need to cover bars, restaurants, cinemas, supermarkets, and so forth, as well as tobacconists. On the other hand, there remains a wide range of products for which stores of one type tend to be dominant, and measurement of what is happening in these stores is adequate for most purposes in establishing what is happening to the product at the retail level. Thus knowledge of how a detergent is moving through foodstores and super-markets would provide an adequate guide to total sales, even though it missed out the sales through pharmacists, hardware stores, depart-ment stores, and other minor outlets.

Where the specification for an audit panel can be formulated in terms of stores of specific types that fit the generally accepted definitions of the *Census of Distribution*, certain advantages are obtained. From the *Census*, information in considerable detail is available about the numbers of stores in the country as well as in local areas, analysed by type of business, form of organization and size, that will help to design samples of stores that are properly related to the numbers and nature of the stores in the area to be covered. On the other hand, if the specification has to be framed in terms of stores stocking a particular product group, there is, at least in the United Kingdom, so far little data available from the *Census* to help with the design of the panel, though some data is available for certain product groups in the 1961 *Census* and some from commercial sample census operations. If, therefore, a panel is to be designed to represent all the stores stocking a particular product group, it may be necessary to carry out quite extensive preliminary research so as to collect the data needed to achieve a proper design. This will be costly, though not necessarily prohibitively so in a small experimental area, but, perhaps of more importance, it will be difficult to project some of the results from the test area on to a wider universe unless comparable data is also available for the larger area.

A second important advantage of the panel specification being made in terms of stores of a defined type is that use can often be made of existing syndicated panels, either in the experimental areas or nation-ally. The national panels are usually offered by research companies operating on a commercial basis, while many local areas suitable for experimental use are covered by panels sponsored by local media owners operating within the areas covered by the local press or tele-vision stations. Where these panels are in operation and are being used simultaneously by numbers of clients, there will be a considerable saving in costs compared with those involved in setting up *ad hoc* panels. There may, of course, be certain disadvantages in using syndicated services, such as possible limitations in the types of store covered and the fact that the times of auditing will be fixed and not open to adapta-tion to particular marketing plans. Conversely, there are in certain areas numbers of panels covering different shop types, so that by using them in combination it is often possible to get something very close to full coverage of a product group while still gaining the financial advantages of syndicated fees.

The size of audit panel necessary will depend on a number of factors, starting with the use to be made of the results. Simple experiments, like feasibility studies or tests to assess whether in-store display material produces any beneficial results, may well be limited to a small number of stores, and each store will be involved in the experimental situation at the same time as providing measures of effect. At the other extreme, where a projectable test-launch, or the effects of an advertising campaign in a town or limited area are being measured, then larger samples of stores will be required, and given proper selection, the larger the panel the more accurate the results will be. The stores included in an audit panel will in this case not be specifically involved in the test, any more than other shops in the same area but outside the panel; normally the panel will contain at least a few shops not even stocking the product concerned.

The extent to which a new product achieves distribution, and the extent to which an existing product being subjected to experimentation holds distribution, will affect the size of the panel needed to provide adequate measures of results. The accuracy with which measures of distribution can be assessed will depend on the total size of the panel, but for those measures concerning physical quantities of goods, the factor determining accuracy will be the number of stores contributing data, i.e. the number of stores handling the product. Thus to measure the sales of a product with 20 per cent distribution will require more shops than would be needed for a product with 80 per cent distribution to give the same level of accuracy.

Another factor affecting panel size is the extent to which stores of the type being sampled vary from one to another. The more similar stores are to each other, the smaller the number needed to provide adequate measures, while the more they vary, the greater the number required. This factor is often linked with the previous one, for the greater the differences between stores, the more likely is it that stocking policies may vary between them and the lower will be the general levels of handling particular brands. In many cases it is possible to design more efficient samples through the use of separate sub-samples for each of the major groups in the population. For example, when sampling food stores, rather than selecting a straight representative panel which might perhaps consist of 70 per cent small stores, 20 per cent medium stores, and 10 per cent supermarkets, a more efficient sample would normally be obtained by weighting the sample by size of outlet and selecting, say, one third supermarkets, one third medium stores, and one third small stores. The imbalance in the sample is corrected at the analysis stage by weighting the three parts back to their proper proportions so as to give unbiased estimates of the overall situation.

The precise size of panel needed for any particular experiment will depend on all of these factors, and probably on others as well in specific situations. Calculations, and knowing what to calculate, call for specialist knowledge and experience, and help should be sought either from the specialist companies who operate panels of this nature or from statisticians experienced in this type of work. However, as a general working rule, it would be unwise to base any audit in a test area on less than thirty stockists of the product concerned. (The obvious exception to this would be where the area being used, either because of its small size or because of the rarity of the shop types involved, itself contains a smaller number of stores.) Among pharmacists in Great Britain, distribution levels of individual brands tend to be above the 80 per cent mark, and most test auditing is done on panels of between thirty and fifty outlets. In the food trade, however, levels of distribution above 50 per cent are not common, particularly among new products, and here most test work is carried out on panels of between 80 and 100 outlets so as to provide adequate numbers of stockists and to allow for the wide variations between small side-street shops and large supermarkets. Where special panels are being set up for an experiment, it may in some cases be possible to limit the costs of the research by recruiting panels with more specific characteristics. Thus a panel set up to measure sales of hair shampoos in grocery stores could well be limited to grocery stores and supermarkets which handle toiletries, thus ensuring that a higher proportion of the shops in the panel will be contributing data, and (given the necessary care in interpreting results) without any loss in the generality of the findings.

To sum up, the value of store audit data is that over time it provides a series of descriptions of the sales of a product and its competitors, backing them up by information on the levels of distribution and stocks and how further supplies are moving into the stores.

Consumer panels

Sales from stores to consumers can be measured in the stores themselves by using retail audit methods, or they can be measured from records of the purchases made by panels of consumers. Basically, a consumer panel consists of a representative sample of consumers, usually housewives, from whom data is collected through time about all their purchases of a range of products.

This data can be collected either through personal calls by field staff, or by post or telephone. When personal calls are used, the field worker visits the selected households at regular intervals (usually weekly for consumer goods, but at longer intervals where only durable or semi-durable goods are being checked) and notes the packages of various products in the house. To supplement this information, the housewife will have been asked to place all the wrappers, cartons, cans, bottles, tubes, etc., of items used up in a special container, which is checked and emptied by the auditor. Then, knowing what was in stock at the previous call, what has appeared on the shelves since, and what has been discarded, a simple calculation shows what has been brought into the household during the period. This technique is frequently known as a home audit, or, more colloquially, as a 'dust-bin check'.

The alternative, and far cheaper, method is to organize the collection of similar data by post by providing members of the panel with diaries in which to enter their purchases in selected commodity groups as they occur. Diaries are usually sent out weekly to last for one week, and various incentives are employed to ensure regular and prompt return of completed diaries to the organizers. Alternatively, for inquiries covering only a limited range of products, telephone interviews can sometimes be used.

These panels, whether operated by post or through personal calls, are expensive to set up and run and are usually operated by specialist research companies who are able to attract large numbers of clients and thus to offer the service at economic fees. Some panels are operated on a national basis, and may be of sufficient size to provide valid samples within large test areas. Others, often sponsored by local advertising media, cover smaller marketing areas more intensively and are suitable for experimental marketing purposes, but they are not as a rule as common as similar store audit facilities. Consequently, it is often found that the requirements of an experiment cannot be met from existing services, and special panels have to be created, and this can be costly, whether the manufacturer himself sets them up or whether he contracts the work out to a specialist agency.

In the past the main use of these panels has been to investigate movements of fast-moving consumer goods, and since these are generally bought by the housewife, she has been the type of person usually signed up for postal panels or contacted during home audits. More recently the methods have been extended to the durable goods field, and here it is usually possible to operate with any responsible member of the household as the main contact. Attempts to extend the use in the opposite direction to take in consumer goods of a personal nature, such as cigarettes, confectionery, cosmetics and toiletries, etc., have not been uniformly successful, and very thorough pilot work is essential in the specific field concerned before use of these methods on items of personal consumption can be recommended for measuring experimental results. The methods can work in these fields, but validity cannot be assumed for these personal items to the extent that it can for the usual run of packaged foods and household products.

Given regular returns of purchases in a product field from a representative sample of the population to be covered, whether housewives, households, or individuals, it becomes possible to provide analyses showing how many people bought each brand of a product group, how much they bought, which pack sizes, probably where they bought it, and how much they paid for it. Given a panel of sufficient size, it is possible to analyse the information by demographic or other meaningful groups so as to show the patterns of use of existing products or the penetration of new launches.

The great advantage of the consumer panel is that it is possible to observe and to follow through time the purchasing patterns of individual members as well as to examine in particular the previous and subsequent purchasing patterns of those members of a panel who purchase a new product, or who buy during the period of an offer, or whose purchasing pattern is affected in any way during a particular marketing operation or experiment. Thus, for example, when a new product is being observed, either during an experimental launch or on a wider basis, it is possible to analyse the number of potential consumers who have actually bought the product, the extent to which they have continued to buy it or have given it up and reverted to an established brand, which brands in the market are being affected, and so forth. Again, given that the panel is of sufficient size, a demographic profile can be established of such various groups as those who have at any point ever bought, bought but given up, or bought and continued to buy.

Size is a major problem with consumer panels. For example, to produce a profile by age or social grade or in any other multi-valued dimension, a minimum of about 100 purchasers will normally be called for. Since few new products are likely to be used by even as many as 20 per cent of the population within two or three months of their introduction, this indicates that panels of at least 500 people will be needed. In many cases, where penetration cannot be expected to reach even the 20 per cent level, still larger panels will be needed before any precise conclusions can be drawn about the characteristics of the group of users. Thus, although the use of these panels offers many attractions during experimental operations, the costs of obtaining the data are likely to be high. If the experiment is taking place in an area already covered by an adequate local panel, or if the area is sufficiently extensive to be broken out from a national panel, then the benefits of syndication are available and the costs are materially reduced. *Ad hoc* panels can, of course, be set up specifically to meet the needs of an experiment, but the whole cost will then fall on the one company involved in the experiment, and the costs will frequently be outside the limits of the available budget. Considering the magnitude of some of the decisions which depend on the results obtained from the experiments, and the sums of money at stake if a wrong decision is reached, failure to provide adequate funds for proper measurements borders on criminal negligence, and there are many companies which should review their responsibilities in setting budgets for marketing experiments generally.

Consumer surveys

The second main area for research during experimental marketing operations is concerned with the flow of information from manufacturer to potential consumers, and may also be concerned with a number of aspects ranging from the initial development of awareness that a product exists at all, through to the development of images, feelings, and beliefs about the product, based in some instances on experience of the product in use, in others merely on the advertising, display, packaging, and so forth.

Two things distinguish this research from the two types discussed above. First, it is not normally possible to use panel methods for this work, since the collection of this information from respondents must condition them in some way and so make them unsuitable for further use in that particular project. Even the most vague general questions aimed at discovering the extent to which respondents have heard of a new product will probably leave some of them with a heightened interest in the product itself or in the product group concerned, which could introduce a degree of atypicality from then on. Once respondents have been questioned on one occasion, whether by personal interview or by telephone or using postal methods, they cannot normally be used again. Panel operations cannot therefore be used, at least at present, though ways of questioning may yet be devised which will make their use possible.

The second distinguishing point in this type of research is the need for very definite specifications of the objectives, first of the stimuli being applied to the population, e.g. advertising, packaging, price, etc., and then of the research objectives. This is vital if adequate results are to be obtained. It does not mean, of course, that other types of research do not need specified objectives, but whereas research into the volume of sales can generally be carried out by either retail or consumer panel methods without the research operators being necessarily aware of the precise targets or objectives involved (though generally it is a good thing if they are), information of this nature is vital if research into awareness and opinions is to be carried out economically and efficiently.

Greatest efficiency is achieved in this area if the creative and the research people can work together from the same creative brief. This should contain information about the target group at whom the various stimuli are to be directed and about the types of response that the stimuli are designed to produce, whether it be awareness of particular product ingredients or attributes, the establishment of beliefs that the product is an improvement over earlier versions or that previous dis-advantages have been overcome, or else such appeals to the emotions as the loving mother who will buy this brand for her children.

Basically, there are so many questions which could be asked about any product, and so many people who could be questioned, that unless attention can be focused on the right people and the right topics, there is every possibility that the specific points which need to be covered if the creative effort is to be evaluated will be missed, or else covered only in so general a way as to be of little use. Hence the need for the research team to know exactly what the creative objectives are so that they can design efficient samples and appropriate questionnaires.

To provide maximum information on the ways in which different measures build up through time, consumer surveys may need to be carried out at intervals during the course of an experiment. In this way not only are the results of the experiment more effectively measured, but more information becomes available on which to base any modifica-tions of the marketing programme which may be beneficial before a move to a wider environment.

Apart from the measures of the less tangible aspects of an experiment, such as awareness and opinions, consumer surveys can also be used to collect data relating to the purchase and use of a product, and this will normally be done even though other research in the form of a consumer panel may be being operated to check more specifically in the same area. This type of information is needed in the first place as a means of further analysis of the survey results, such as the analysis of opinion data according to whether the respondent has personally bought and used the product or whether he is merely influenced by other factors. For many products, more detailed information can be collected to cover such data as the frequency of purchase, how long the current brand has been used, what brand was previously used, and so forth. This information is useful for grouping respondents for analysis purposes, and if consumer panel data is not available, it may go some way towards filling the gap, though it can seldom form a complete substitute for the more detailed information on consumer purchasing habits that panels provide. Conversely, panels can never be used for collecting the awareness and opinion data provided by consumer surveys.

Because consumer surveys are normally designed to meet specific needs relating to a particular experiment, they are usually carried out on an *ad hoc* basis, and so there are fewer syndicated facilities than in the case of the panel methods. However, there are increasing numbers of syndicated facilities becoming available, either in areas covered by local media or covering wider areas which can sometimes be divided for experimental purposes. As with panels, the use of syndicated facilities will reduce the costs of research, but such savings may have to be balanced against a less specific sample design, the acceptance of a set of timings which may not be optimal for the experiment, or other possible constraints.

Other methods

Other methods of research and measurement may be appropriate for some experiments, and may either exist as established services or else need to be set up on an *ad hoc* basis.

Among established services are a number which operate mainly to provide running checks on existing products, giving various measures of brand performance or acceptance obtained from some form of omnibus survey. Variants or combinations of panels and *ad hoc* surveys, personal or telephone interviews, postal questionnaires and diaries, are used to provide series of indices which are frequently marketed under 'brand names', such as ACCESS or the TGI in Great Britain, or the BRI in the United States. Where such facilities exist, they should be investigated to establish whether they can be used in an experimental situation, such benefits as lower costs and the availability of back data being assessed against whatever limitations and constraints may be imposed.

In other cases, an experiment may call for direct observation, photographic records, the use of time-lapse cameras, analyses of samples of retail credit customers, and so forth. These situations generally call for the development of combinations of techniques exclusively for one series of experiments, and it must be left to the creative flair of the experimenter or to the consultants whom he employs to deal with the problems.

The choice of methods of measurement

The prime factor governing which methods of measurement should be used will, of course, be the nature of the experiment.

In any experiment, factors are varied in the expectation that, through a longer or shorter sequence of events, a change will be effected in the level of sales, profitability, or whatever criterion is being used. It is not normally possible to measure a change in the level of profit directly from a test in a small area, but only to make an assessment of changes based on changes in the volume of sales. Hence, in most cases, the ultimate benefit of any change tends to be measured in terms of sales, either as sales out of shops, measured through a store audit, or purchases made by consumers measured on, say, a panel of housewives.

Such assessments of sales levels and changes in them are sufficient if only a 'go, no-go' decision or a projection of sales is required. This data is also adequate in the case of experiments which show completely successful results, but where the outcome has been less successful more information is needed at intermediate stages between the stimulus and final sales if any attempts are to be made to diagnose the causes and take remedial action.

For simple experiments, it may be possible to select one research mechanism to provide all the data necessary for both assessment and diagnosis, but in more complex cases – and in projectable test launching in particular – the research should cover the full range of possible effects. It should then have regard to both the physical flow of goods from the manufacturer to the wholesaler or warehouse and on to the retail store and consumer, as well as the flow of information leading to the development of awareness and opinions and, possibly, use of the product.

In these cases, there should be little question of choosing between the research measures available, since, for a full appreciation of the outcome of an experiment and its implications for future plans, measurements at each and every stage should be organized if at all possible. All too often full use cannot be made of experimental results because certain measurements have not been included and no detail is available. It may, therefore, become impossible either to determine the causes which have led to the failure of a particular experiment or venture or to detect areas of weakness where, even in successful experiments, some change or adjustment could lead to an improved performance.

When considering the reliability or accuracy of panel operations, whether they are concerned with measurements in stores or among consumers, it should be remembered that the problem has two dimensions – one concerned with absolute levels and the other with any trend. The appropriate dimension must be used in any particular experiment.

Consider the results from a panel of either stores or individuals. A simple statistic, such as the number of packets of a product purchased during a given period, will be subject to some degree of sampling error, owing to the fact that a sample of whatever size will generate readings which depart from the true but generally unknown value. The size of this error will in general depend on the precise nature of the sample concerned, and will tend to be much the same in successive periods of time. Thus, if the June reading has an error of this type in it of 3 per cent, the figure for July is likely to be in error to much the same extent, irrespective of how the market has moved.

If the object of the experiment is to find out how far a course of action affects the sales of an existing product, then the fact that the sampling error will remain fairly constant from month to month is an advantage because a greater proportion of any apparent movement will then be real and comparatively small shifts may well be significant. If, instead of a panel, independent samples have been used on each occasion, each sample will be subject to its own sampling error, and the effects of these will be cumulative; they can thus become large in comparison with the real changes being sought, swamping them and making the results insignificant. Therefore panels enable more precise readings to be made of situations in which a change is being measured in the performance of an existing brand. This aspect is considered in more detail in the next chapter.

When the experiment is concerned with test-launching a new product, the problem is not only to detect whether the measurements being made have moved from one period to the next, but also to determine how high the figures for the new product will rise. In this case, although a series of readings is being generated, the absolute level at which the product settles is being read from the sample as an absolute figure and will contain the full sampling error to which that particular sample or panel is subject. Thus there is no gain in accuracy to be had from using a panel when an absolute measurement of a level is required as against measuring changes in relative levels, although clearly there are other good reasons for using panels, including the type of information that can be obtained from direct recording of quantities.

9

The assessment of results

The reliability of any projections made from an experimental area on to a wider market depends both on the precision with which the experimental measurements are made and on the strength of the relationships between the experimental situation and the wider market used in framing projections. This chapter deals with the precision of the experimental measurements and leaves the development of projections and forecasts until Chapter 10.

Four factors in general determine the precision of measurements in an experiment: (a) the nature of the statistic being measured, (b) the size of the sample of observations, (c) the method of sampling, and (d) the method of measurement.

Attributes and variables

Measurements basically fall into two categories: (a) measurements of attributes and (b) measurements of variables. Attributes include such factors as being aware of a product, stocking it, being in a particular occupation group or social class, and so forth, and results concerned with attributes are generally expressed in proportions or percentages, e.g. 47 per cent of people being aware of a product, or 78 per cent of shops stocking it. Variables include such items as the number of cans of soup purchased by a housewife in a month, the number of eggs sold by a shop in a week, or the number of pounds of butter in stock at the end of a month. Some measurements, such as age, are strictly variables, but belonging to a particular age group, as, say, 35–44, is treated as an attribute, and other variables may be used from time to time to form groupings that can be treated as attributes, such as dividing purchasers of a product into light, medium, or heavy buyers according to the quantities bought during a period.

Standard error of an attribute

The accuracy or precision of a result derived from an inquiry based on sampling procedures is expressed in terms of the 'standard error' of the estimate, which is derived by calculation from the data. The term is unfortunate, since in ordinary language an error is a mistake, but it has become strongly established.

When dealing with statistics of attributes derived from simple random sampling, the standard error attaching to a particular result can be calculated very easily. The proportion of the sample possessing the attribute is denoted by p, and the proportion not possessing the attribute by q. (Hence $p + q = 1$, or $q = 1 - p$.) If the number of items in the sample is n, then the standard error of p, denoted by s.e., is:

$$\text{s.e.} = \sqrt{\frac{pq}{n}}$$

If, for example, a survey among 400 shops selected by simple random sampling shows 80 per cent carrying stocks of a product, the standard error of the estimate of 80 per cent is given by:

$$\text{s.e.} = \sqrt{\frac{\cdot 8 \times \cdot 2}{400}}$$

$$= \sqrt{\frac{\cdot 16}{400}}$$

$$= \frac{\cdot 4}{20}$$

$$= \pm \cdot 02, \text{ or } = \pm 2\%$$

This figure is in no sense an absolute limit to the range of error, but is merely a measure of the degree of error or variation to which the estimate is subject. There is no theoretical reason why, if enough samples

Figure 9.1

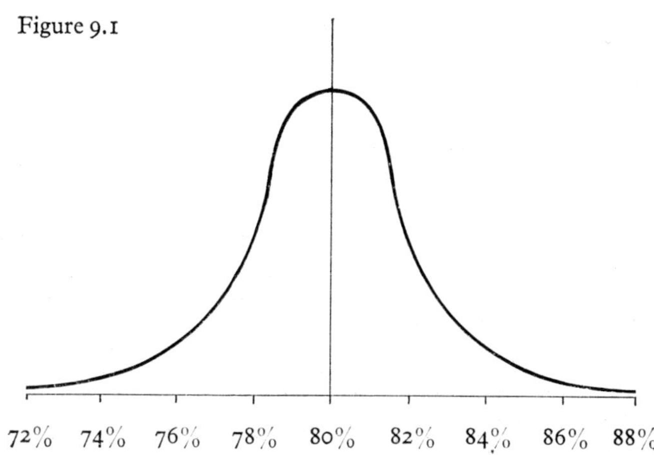

of 400 shops were taken and all were measured simultaneously, all thus measuring the same situation, some of the samples should not produce estimates of the percentage stocking the product to be as low as 50 per cent or less or as high as 100 per cent. The chances of obtaining such extreme results, however, are very low, and one would have to be very unlucky to get them if the true value was, say, 80 per cent. The estimated values from a whole series of samples of 400 from a population where the true value was 80 per cent would form the pattern shown in Figure 9.1, with most of the estimates closely grouped around 80 per cent and results far removed from the true value being less frequent.

The 95 per cent limits

The standard error provides a description of the form of the error curve, which for samples of the sizes normally used in this type of work conforms to certain rules. The most frequently used rule is that 95 per cent of the results of the samples will fall within a range of plus or minus twice the standard error, hence the term '95 per cent limits'. Thus, if the true level of distribution of the product is 80 per cent, then nineteen times out of twenty the result obtained from a simple random sample of 400 shops will fall within the range of 80 per cent $\pm$ 2 $\times$ 2 per cent, cr within the range of 76 to 84 per cent. By a slight inversion of the reasoning, which will be acceptable for all practical purposes, we can then move on to say that if a single sample of 400 shops shows 80 per cent stocking a product, the true figure will ninety-five times out of a hundred lie within the range of 76 to 84 per cent.

The practice of taking the 95 per cent limits is a workable compromise between taking a narrower band, that would give a false impression of precision, since results would often fall outside the limits, and taking a wider band at, for instance, 99 per cent, that would then include more extreme results that would only occur once in a hundred times. The choice of the 95 per cent level is reputed to have been made in the first place by an early and eminent statistician who, faced with the problem of setting limits to some experimental results, wandered off into the woods for some hours before returning and saying that the 95 per cent level was the one to use. His choice has stood the test of time.

This simple method of calculating the standard error of percentages or proportions is not strictly valid when assessing the results of most market research inquiries, since they are not normally based upon simple random samples. Most samples cease to be simple as, to increase the cost efficiency of field work, contacts are clustered and selected by 'multi-stage' sampling processes. They may also be stratified in some way, as by area, age, or sex for samples of individuals, or by store type for retail outlets, and the samples may also be weighted. Many samples are not random because other methods of selecting the units, like quota sampling, have been used. The effect of stratification and weighting will generally be to reduce the standard error below the level obtained through the simple calculation, while the use of multi-stage sample designs and other departures from simple random methods will tend to increase the error. The two sets of influences will to some extent tend to offset each other, and the calculated figure may be taken as a rough guide to the standard error of a result, though the more prudent may be inclined to increase the calculated figures by a quarter or a half before applying them.

Where it is vital to have a more precise calculation of the standard error, this can be made from the raw data, taking account of the strata into which the units are divided and any weighting which is used. This can be a laborious calculation, but the increasing use of computers is easing the problem. The procedures depend on the original design of the sample, and the detailed calculations are beyond the scope of this book.

Calculation of required sample size

Since the rough calculation of the standard error (s.e.) of an attribute depends only on the percentage having or not having the attribute being measured and on the sample size, it is possible in most cases to form some assessment of the standard error to be expected before the survey is carried out by using estimates of the percentages likely to be obtained and putting them in the formula above. It is then possible to insert a proposed value for the sample size, n, and to calculate the standard error which will emerge; or, to insert some specific value of s.e. to give a required degree of precision, and to calculate the value of n required to achieve it.

Suppose it is anticipated that, by a certain time after its launch, a new product will have been bought at least once by 30 per cent of house-wives. How large a sample will be required to determine this within ± 3 per cent, taking the 95 per cent limits? Here it is estimated that:

$$p = \cdot 3$$
$$q = \cdot 7$$

and required that

$$\text{s.e.} = \cdot 015 \text{ or less}$$

Substituting these values in the formula:

$$\text{s.e.} = \sqrt{\frac{pq}{n}}$$

$$\cdot 015 = \sqrt{\frac{\cdot 3 \times \cdot 7}{n}}$$

$$n = \frac{\cdot 21}{\cdot 015^2}$$

$$n = 933$$

Hence, to obtain the measurements required, a sample of about 950 housewives will need to be interviewed.

Clearly the precision of a result can be increased or decreased by changing n, the number in the sample, but it should be noted that it is $\sqrt{n}$ which enters into the formula, so that to halve the range of error the sample must be quadrupled, and so on.

If, within the main sample, it is necessary to assess the standard error of one part, say of housewives under thirty-five years of age, then the same calculation will give the same rough indication of the range of error, based on the number n' of interviews in that cell. Consequently it is usually the limits of accuracy demanded from such sub-samples as age groups or class groups which determine the overall size of samples used, rather than the degree of precision required in the total sample itself.

The coefficient of variation

One way of considering the variation or error in sampling results is to express the standard error as a percentage of the estimated value itself. This percentage is known as the coefficient of variation (CV), and for statistics of attributes it is simply estimated thus:

$$\text{CV} = \frac{\text{s.e.}}{p} \times 100\%$$

This is a useful shorthand way of expressing the results, especially if they are grossed up to some population figure. Suppose that the results quoted on the distribution of a product among a sample of 400 shops applied to an area in which there were 9,350 shops, then 80 per cent of this figure would come to 7,480. The coefficient of variation would be:

$$\frac{\cdot 02}{\cdot 80} \times 100\% = 2 \cdot 5\%$$

Taking twice this figure in the same way as we use twice the standard error, the estimated number of shops in the whole area stocking the product can be expressed as 7,480 $\pm$ 5 per cent, which immediately conveys a clear idea of the estimate's precision.

Standard error of a variable

The factor which makes attributes comparatively simple to handle in statistical terms is that the reading from any one member of the sample, whether it is an individual, a store or whatever, counts as one if the member has the attribute being measured and as zero if it is absent. If, then, we know the value of p, either as a proportion or as a percentage, we automatically know the whole composition of the sample in terms of zeros and ones. When measurement of a variable is involved, however, this ceases to be the case, and values other than 0 and 1 are likely to be recorded.

Consider a product bought by housewives, packets of tea, for example, where, depending on the size of the family and its habits, purchases during a month may range from zero packets to a dozen or more. The calculation of the average quantity bought per household, say m, gives no indication of the extent of variation between buyers and does not in itself indicate how many housewives bought 0, 1, 2, 3, etc., packets in the month. Neither does it lead us directly to a method of calculating the standard error. This can only be done directly by going back to the data itself and calculating first the standard deviation (s.d.) and then the standard error.

Briefly, for a simple random sample the standard deviation is calculated by summing the squares of the differences between each reading and the mean, dividing by the number in the sample, and taking the square root. This is more elegantly expressed by the formula:

$$\text{s.d.} = \sqrt{\frac{1}{n} \sum (x - m)^2}$$

where n = the number in the sample

m = the average quantity in the whole sample

x = the quantity bought by each individual, taken in turn

$\sum$ = the Greek letter 'sigma' indicating that all the squares of the deviations are to be summed together.

To obtain the standard error to indicate the precision of the average m the standard deviation is divided by the square root of n. This gives:

$$\text{s.e.} = \frac{\text{s.d.}}{\sqrt{n}} \text{ or } \sqrt{\frac{\text{s.d.}^2}{n}}$$

In cases where the pattern of purchases is skewed – that is, as is commonly the case, where large numbers of people buy zero or small quantities and where only small numbers buy large quantities – these calculations should only be made where n is greater than 100, otherwise the skewness of the original data will tend to distort the calculated value of the standard error.

Short-cut calculations

The calculation of the standard errors attaching to estimates concerning variables is a complex matter if undertaken from the data itself, but there are short cuts that can often be employed.

Consider the results of a survey or of a panel operation to discover the average purchases of the large size of a product in a month by housewives in an area. The results show some housewives with the attribute of having bought the product in the month, and some who did not buy. The proportion buying can be defined as p. Among this proportion, the average number of packets bought per buyer may be calculated and called w. The average purchases among all housewives, including the non-buyers with zero purchases, is m, and is the figure usually required in, for example, making an estimate of the total purchases by housewives in the area. These three statistics, p, w, and m, are related by the following formula:

$$m = p.w$$

Now, it may be shown that the coefficients of variation of these three statistics are related in the following way:

$$CV_m^2 = CV_p^2 + CV_w^2$$

and consequently the coefficient of variation of m can never be less than either of the other two. It cannot be less than CV_p whatever the value of CV_w, and CV_p is comparatively easy to calculate given either p from the sample or some prior estimate of it.

If a sample of 1,000 housewives showed that 200 bought the product in a period of a month, then $p = \cdot2$ and the standard error of p is:

$$\text{s.e.}_p = \sqrt{\frac{\cdot2 \times \cdot8}{1,000}}$$

$$= \cdot0126$$

Then:

$$CV_p = \frac{\cdot0126}{\cdot2}$$

$$= \cdot063 \text{ or } 6\cdot3\%$$

Since the coefficient of variation of p is therefore $6\cdot3$ per cent, it follows that the coefficient of variation of m, the average quantity bought calculated over all housewives in the sample, must be greater than 6·3 per cent, giving 95 per cent limits of about $12\frac{1}{2}$ per cent as a minimum. This means that the calculated value of m has minimum 95 per cent limits of error of $\pm 12\frac{1}{2}$ per cent of m.

It is, in fact, possible to go further than this with samples of housewives, since it is known that the distribution of quantities bought follows certain patterns, and Chatsfield, Ehrenberg and Goodhardt have shown that an approximation to the standard deviation of the purchases is given by $1·7\,(w-1)$.* Hence, if w is known or can be assessed in advance, its standard error and coefficient of variation can be estimated.

Suppose that among the sample of 1,000 housewives used above, the average rate of buying in a month, m, was two thirds of a packet. Then:

$$m = p.w$$
$$·67 = ·2w$$
$$w = 3·35$$
$$\text{s.d.}_w = 1·7\,(w-1)$$
$$= 1·7 \times 2·35$$
$$= 3·995$$

Now, w is the average quantity bought by purchasers of the product, of whom there were 20 per cent in 1,000, so the calculation of w has been based on a sub-sample of 200 housewives. Hence:

$$\text{s.e.}_w = \frac{3·995}{\sqrt{200}}$$
$$= ·283$$

Hence:

$$\text{CV}_w = \frac{·283}{3·35}$$
$$= ·085 \text{ or } 8·5\%$$

Now:

$$\text{CV}_m^2 = \text{CV}_p^2 + \text{CV}_w^2$$
$$= ·063^2 + ·085^2$$
$$= ·003969 + ·007225$$
$$= ·011194$$
$$\therefore \text{CV}_m = ·105, \text{ or } 10·5\%$$

Hence:

$$\text{s.e.}_m = m \times \text{CV}_m$$
$$= ·67 \times ·105$$
$$= ·0703 \text{ packets}$$

* See Further Reading, page 184.

Hence this approximate method of calculation shows that the 95 per cent limits of m, the average quantity bought in this example, are $\cdot 67 \pm \cdot 14$ packets.

This method may appear somewhat roundabout and cumbersome, but it is far quicker and easier than calculating the same figures from raw data. More important in most cases, the calculations can be made using only the figures of the proportions of housewives buying the product and the average quantity bought which appear in the normal research reports, or they can be made in advance of the research on estimates of the likely results. The results are only approximate, because they take no account of departures from simple random sampling – through the methods of sample selection or stratification – but they will probably provide a fair guide to the situation.

The overall relationship used here between the coefficients of variation applies also to data obtained from store audits, but there are difficulties about the separate parts of the calculation. The value of p is given by the proportion of stores handling or stocking a product in a period (calculated on a store basis and not on a volume basis), and if this is fairly consistent between categories of stores – multiples, co-operatives, group members, etc. – then the calculation of CV_p can be made with some confidence. If, however, as not infrequently happens as a result of manufacturers' distribution policies, stores' own-lable policies, etc., there are wide differences between distribution levels between different types of store, any calculation based solely on the overall level of p is likely to lead to bias.

The calculations concerning w in terms of sales per shop handling or similar statistics, are not possible because little has been published on the form of their patterns and there is no simple formula for estimating the standard deviation from w itself. Even if it existed, the marked differences which tend to occur in w between different categories of stores might still prevent it being of any use in working from overall figures unless full account is taken of the stratification and weighting of the sample, which are generally far more marked in this area than in housewife panels. Therefore calculations of the sampling errors in store panels must be carried out on the original data collected from the outlets.

Standard errors of differences

Discussion so far has been concerned only with the precision of such single results as the rate of sale of a new product after six months on the market or the proportion of people aware of a product at one point in time. Frequently, however, the assessment of experimental results depends on a comparison being made between two or more values derived from different points in time, as with before-and-after experiments; from different areas when two or more alternatives are being tested; or from both together. But if each separate reading is subject to sampling error, how far are any differences between them real and how far may they be due to chance fluctuations in the samples?

Two basic sets of conditions need to be distinguished, depending on the method by which the data were collected. If each statistic, such as the proportion of housewives who bought the product in a month, has been obtained from a separate sample of housewives, then the two estimates are independent. If the comparison is between the proportions buying in each of two areas, then separate samples must automatically be used, and the results are again independent. If the readings are for the same area at different points in time, they may have been obtained by using different samples on each occasion, and in this case results will still be independent; but if there are two readings that have been obtained from the same panel of contacts at the two points in time, then the samples are not independent since the same people were used and the results obtained are likely to be correlated.

Independent samples

The measure used to assess whether an observed difference between two values of a statistic is real and beyond the bounds of chance fluctuations is the standard error of the difference. For independent samples, this is simply the square root of the sum of the squares of the two separate standard errors. If two proportions are to be compared, p_1, and p_2, or two means, m_1 and m_2, the standard error of the difference between them is:

$$\text{s.e.}_d = \sqrt{\text{s.e.}_1^2 + \text{s.e.}_2^2}$$

Here s.e._d is the standard error of the difference, where the samples are independent, and it is calculated in the same way for both proportions and averages.

Measurements from the same sample

When successive measurements are made on the same sample of people or stores, usually through standing panels from which data is collected at regular intervals, the calculation involves another factor, the correlation coefficient. This is a measure of the extent to which readings made on the two occasions are related through being obtained from the same source.

In using a panel, any single measurement is subject to sampling error just as it would be for an *ad hoc* sample. The sample may contain, by chance, either too many heavy buyers, so leading to an overestimate of the average purchases, or too many light buyers or non-buyers, having a reverse effect. When the second or subsequent set of data is collected, then it is to be expected, at least for most products frequently bought and in common use, that these people will still tend to behave in the same way and that the panel will still contain about the same aberrant numbers of light or heavy buyers. Thus the standard error in the second set of data will be dependent upon, or similar to, the error in the first set. The extent to which sampling error will swing about from one period to the next is thus reduced below the level of swings expected between independent samples, and so the standard error of the difference between two results is similarly reduced. It is damped down to the extent that the members of the panel behave consistently between one period and another, and the measure of this consistency is the correlation coefficient.

If the members of the panel were quite consistent between one period and another, with only those who bought in the first period buying in the second and all those who bought heavily buying heavily in both periods, and so on, the correlation coefficient between the two periods would be 1·0. If, however, everyone behaved erratically, and behaviour in one period was no guide to behaviour in the next, so that a heavy buyer in one period might equally well become a light or a non-buyer as remain a heavy buyer in the second period, the relationship would break down and the correlation coefficient would be zero. Finally, as can happen in markets where the purchase interval is long, it may be found that a reverse relationship exists where, almost automatically, those buying in one period do not buy in the next while the non-buyers become buyers. Here the correlation coefficient would be reversed and take a value approaching −1·0.

The calculation of the standard error of a difference using panel data now becomes:

$$\text{s.e.}_d = \sqrt{\text{s.e.}_1^2 + \text{s.e.}_2^2 - 2r(\text{s.e.}_1 \times \text{s.e.}_2)}$$

In this equation r is the coefficient of correlation. If r is positive, indicating consistency in behaviour among panel members from one period to the next, then the standard error of the difference is reduced below the level for independent samples. If r is zero, indicating that results in one period are independent of results in the next, the standard error is the same as for independent samples. In the rare event of r being negative, the standard error is increased above the level of independent samples, but this eventuality need be of no concern where frequently purchased goods are being measured.

The value of r can only be calculated from the original data, and must be calculated in relation to the statistic being assessed, the value obtained depending on the state of the market concerned. If the market is highly volatile and there is little brand loyalty, correlation between purchasers in one period and in the next may be low, but in more normal markets, with only a moderate degree of switching, correlations will be higher. As an example, consider a brand bought by 20 per cent of housewives in one period and 22 per cent in the next, with 16 per cent buying in both periods, 4 per cent buying in the first but not in the second, 6 per cent buying in the second who did not buy in the first, so leaving 74 per cent not buying in either period. The correlation coefficient can be calculated here to be $+0.7$, and for a panel of 1,000 housewives, the calculation of the standard error of the difference between the proportions buying in each period is as follows:

$$\text{s.e.}_d = \sqrt{\frac{\cdot1600}{1,000} + \frac{\cdot1716}{1,000} - \frac{2 \times 0.7 \times \cdot4 \times \cdot414}{1,000}}$$

$$= \sqrt{\cdot0000998}$$

$$= \cdot01 \text{ or } 1\%$$

If the data available had been collected from two independent samples instead of from a panel, the standard error of the same difference would have been:

$$\text{s.e.}_d = \sqrt{\frac{\cdot1600}{1,000} + \frac{\cdot1716}{1,000}}$$

$$= \sqrt{\cdot0003316}$$

$$= \cdot018 \text{ or } 1\cdot8\%$$

Therefore the use of a panel has almost halved the standard error of the difference between the two results.

The significance of differences

This standard error of the difference can be regarded in the same way as individual standard errors, in that a difference of twice the standard error is only likely to arise by chance on 5 per cent of occasions, and differences which exceed this limit of twice the standard error are termed 'significant' at the 5 per cent level. Differences which are three times as large as the standard error would only arise by chance less than once in a hundred occasions, and these are termed significant at the 1 per cent level. Conversely, differences equal to one standard error can be expected to occur by chance alone about 30 per cent of the time, and such results can be described as significant at the 30 per cent level.

The 5 per cent level of significance is the one most widely used, and it normally forms a fair compromise between the risk of accepting as real a set of results only due to chance and the opposite risk of setting such stringent standards that some real differences will be rejected because they do not reach them. Ideally, limits should be set for each experiment in the context of the risks inherent in the situation. If the risks involved in adopting the experimental project more widely are high, so that virtual certainty of a successful outcome is demanded before any decision to proceed can be safely taken, the 1 per cent level should be used in preference to the 5 per cent level. If, however, the risks are lower, and all that is being sought is reasonable assurance that success is more likely than failure, then the 30 per cent limits would suffice.

The fact that the outcome of an experiment is not significant does not in itself mean that there is no difference between the two situations under comparison, but merely that the methods used have not been sufficiently powerful to disentangle any real movement from the possible chance movements inherent in a situation. Any observed difference between the measurements of the two situations remains the 'best' estimate of the real difference, but those below the required level of significance are deemed too unreliable for further action.

Consider a test involving two campaigns designed to create awareness of some new product attribute. Each campaign is run in a separate television area and samples of 400 housewives are interviewed in each area. The results show that awareness in one area is at a 50 per cent level and in the other at 60 per cent. How should these results be assessed?

The difference between the two readings, expressed in proportions, is $\cdot 60 - \cdot 50 = \cdot 10$. The standard error of the difference between independent samples is calculated as follows:

$$\begin{aligned} \text{s.e.}_d &= \sqrt{\text{s.e.}_1{}^2 + \text{s.e.}_2{}^2} \\ &= \sqrt{\frac{\cdot 5 \times \cdot 5}{400} + \frac{\cdot 6 \times \cdot 4}{400}} \\ &= \sqrt{\frac{\cdot 49}{400}} \\ &= \sqrt{\cdot 001225} \\ &= \cdot 035 \text{ or } 3\tfrac{1}{2}\% \end{aligned}$$

Now the difference of $\cdot 10$ between the two readings is just under three times the sampling error of the difference at $\cdot 035$, so that the observed difference is significant and there is less than one chance in a hundred that it is merely due to sampling effects.

An alternative and often useful way of looking at the results is as follows. Suppose that the 5 per cent significance level has been accepted as sufficiently rigorous for the experiment. This calls for a difference between the two observations of twice the standard error, i.e. twice $3\frac{1}{2}$ per cent. But the observed difference is 10 per cent, which leaves 3 per cent spare after the required significance level has been reached, indicating that there is only a one in twenty chance of the difference being as low as 3 per cent.

As with the calculations of the simple standard error attaching to a single reading, the formula for calculating the standard error of a difference can either be used after the event to assess the meaning of results already obtained, or else to make prior calculation of the sample sizes needed to meet specific requirements.

Comparisons with control areas

When a control area as well as an experimental area is used and measurements are made before and after the introduction of the experimental project, there are four measurements and two differences to be considered. The crux of the matter will be whether the differences observed over time in the two areas differ significantly from each other, or whether any variation between them could be merely due to chance alone.

When the samples are independent, the standard error of the difference between two differences is itself the square root of the sum of the squares of the standard errors of the individual differences, which can be verified as the square root of the sum of the squares of the standard errors of all the four readings. This again is more easily expressed in symbols.

Let:

$$a_1 \text{ and } a_2 = \text{the two measurements in the experimental area}$$
$$b_1 \text{ and } b_2 = \text{the two measurements in the control area}$$

The difference between any changes in the two areas is:

$$d = (a_2 - a_1) - (b_2 - b_1)$$

and for independent samples:

$$\text{s.e.}_d = \sqrt{\text{s.e.}_{a2}^2 + \text{s.e.}_{a1}^2 + \text{s.e.}_{b2}^2 + \text{s.e.}_{b1}^2}$$

An alternative approach is to consider whether the difference between the pair of readings after the test is significantly greater than the difference between the earlier pair. The difference to be tested is then in the form:

$$d' = (a_2 - b_2) - (a_1 - b_1)$$
$$= a_2 - a_1 - b_2 + b_1$$
$$= (a_2 - a_1) - (b_2 - b_1)$$
$$= d \text{ above}$$

The calculation of the standard error is therefore the same whether it is differences in readings between areas or between times that are being compared.

With panels where the samples are not independent, the correlations between a_1 and a_2 and between b_1 and b_2 appear in the formula as they do in the case of the direct comparisons between pairs. As there will be no correlation between the panels in one area and another, no further correlation coefficients are involved.

Series of measurements

When panels are used, whether of stores or consumers, there will normally be a series of readings during the course of an experiment. The significance of the difference between any pair of these readings can be assessed by using the methods already outlined for panels and by using the appropriate correlation coefficient, but extending the assessment to series of readings is a more complex operation which cannot be covered in this book. There is, however, one simple device which is often useful.

If there is no trend in the statistics being studied, that is, if the proportions of housewives using a product or the rate of sale out of stores is steady, the fluctuations in the levels recorded by a panel will be equally divided between upward and downward movements. The probability that the next movement from a given time will be upwards will be $\frac{1}{2}$. It follows from the normal rules governing probabilities that the chance of two upward movements in succession is $\frac{1}{4}$, of three in succession is $\frac{1}{8}$, and of four in succession $\frac{1}{16}$. Given then that the original series of data was stationary before the introduction of the experiment, a subsequent run of four upward (or four downward) movements in the data in succession would only occur by chance once in sixteen times, or on 6 per cent of occasions. Thus four similar movements in succession from a stationary starting-point can be taken as significant at the 6 per cent level. This is a somewhat crude method of assessment, but it is useful when no other methods are available and is independent of the size of samples used.

Where trends exist in the data, whether seasonal or longer-term, a control area should, of course, be used. If the two areas have been following similar patterns prior to the experiment, then the method can with care be applied to the relative sizes of the movements between the two panels. Assuming that it is chance whether, under non-experimental conditions, the movement in the experimental area is larger or smaller than the corresponding movement in the control area, then the same series of probabilities applies and a run of four larger movements in the experimental area becomes significant at the 6 per cent level. Some care is needed, however, to ensure that the inherent variation between successive panel readings is similar in each area before the experiment is started, or, if they are different, that steps will be taken to standardize the data before applying this test.

Further complications

There is far more to the problem of assessing the significance of differences between sample results than these few simple formulae. There are other types of statistical tests which can be applied which make use of far more of the data than the percentages and means discussed here; and there are refinements in the ways of using even these simple formulae.

The formulae in this chapter will provide a basis for understanding something about tests of significance, and in general little harm will come from using these methods in simple experiments. Even with apparently simple tests, however, there are pitfalls which will lead to errors or to waste if they are not recognized. Discussion of all the possible complications goes beyond the scope of this chapter, but the following comparison between two similar situations illustrates one point which is not always appreciated.

Two campaigns, A and B, are to be run in separate areas and measurements made to assess their effects in creating awareness of a new product. Now if the objective is to find out which campaign leads to the higher level of awareness the test on page 134 is appropriate. This is known as a 'two-tailed' test and it operates whether A performs better than B, or B better than A, and is designed so that if the margin between the two results is large enough *either* way, the difference will emerge as significant. If however the problem is to find out specifically whether *A is better than B*, a different form of the test known as a 'one-tailed' test becomes appropriate and in this case significance at the 95 per cent level is achieved if the difference is only 1·6 times the standard error. In this second case the test is designed only to assess whether an observed margin of A over B is significant.

This point is by no means merely of academic interest, because the sample sizes required in one-tailed tests need be only about two-thirds the size of those for two-tailed tests, for the same degree of precision. Two points follow from this. First, the methods which will be used to analyse the data need to be decided at a very early stage if the operation is to be planned efficiently and economically; and second, expert help should be sought from the beginning of the experiment.

Early assessment of results

There is one final topic which deserves mention in this chapter, and that is a technique for making an early assessment of the results of an experiment from the first few readings from a consumer panel. This is particularly valuable in launching new products, whether experimentally or in the wider market, but it is also useful when making changes to the mix of an existing product. The three measurements used to make the assessment have been described by Parfitt and Collins, following earlier work by Baum and Dennis.*

The first measure is the cumulative penetration of the brand expressed as a percentage of the cumulative penetration of the product group. Each panel member buying the brand for the first time adds one to the cumulative penetration, and a plot of this figure percentaged on the cumulative number of buyers in the product field tends to follow a regular pattern, approximately like a flattened 's'.

Figure 9.2

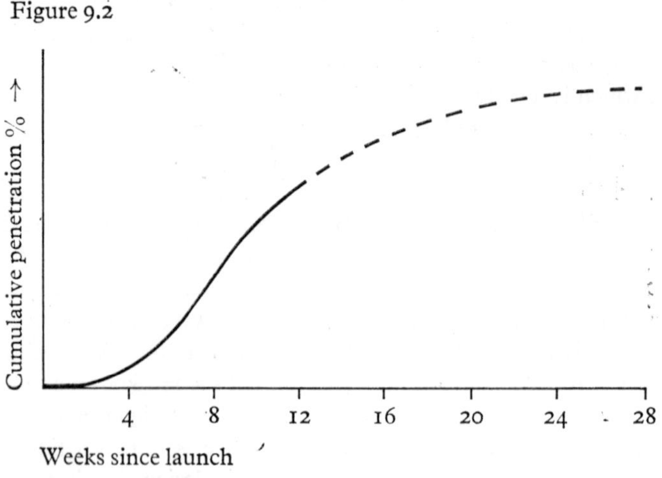

* See Further Reading, page 184

Once the pattern has developed to a stage where the line begins to level off, it is possible to project it mathematically and to obtain an estimate of the level it will achieve when it reaches its maximum. It will, in fact, continue to grow very slowly, but this does not affect the issue.

The second measure is the share of the market taken by the brand among those housewives who have ever bought it, as the time from their initial purchase increases. To obtain this measure, the purchases of the brand and its competitors are not, as is normally done, analysed by calendar weeks, but by elapsed weeks from the initial purchase by the housewife. The result is a series of brand shares achieved among housewives in weeks 1, 2, 3, etc., after each made her first purchase, and this again tends to follow a regular pattern which can be projected mathematically to a stable level (Figure 9.3).

Figure 9.3

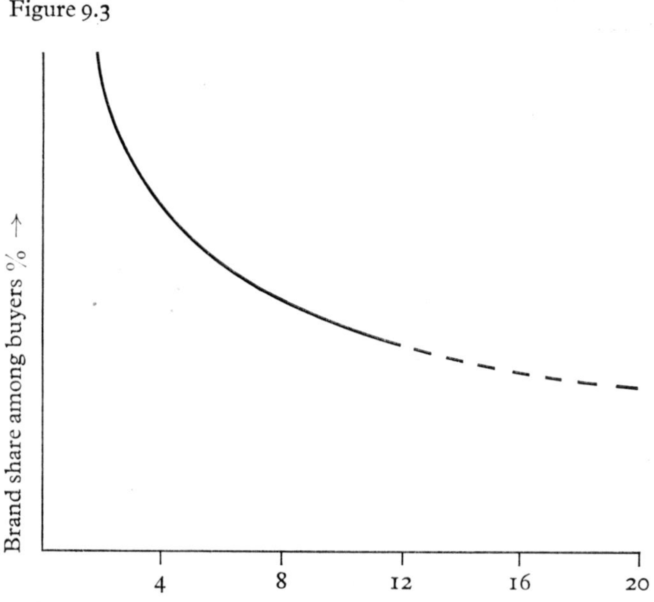

If these two figures of the expected stable levels of the cumulative penetration among users of the product group, and of the brand share gained among purchasers in their subsequent purchases, are expressed as percentages and multiplied together, the result will be a fair indication of the level of brand share at which the product will settle.

The third measure adds a refinement to the calculation, and is the ratio between the rate of buying in the product field of triers of the new brand and the rate of buying in the field of all buyers. If the new product has attracted heavy buyers, then this ratio will be greater than one; if predominantly light buyers have been attracted, it will be less than one.

Multiplication of the first assessment of brand share by this ratio adds a refinement in that the rate of buying by purchasers of the new brand is taken into account. The final assessment then is:

Estimated stable share $= p.s.w$

where $p =$ projected cumulative penetration

$s =$ projected share of repurchases

$w =$ buying ratio

This method can also be applied to changes in the mix of existing products by analysis of the period prior to any change to establish the existing stable levels, and plotting and projecting any changes resulting from the new activity.

Projections, predictions and forecasts

The ultimate objective in carrying out a projectable experiment is to produce a forecast of what is likely to happen if the experimental factors are introduced into other marketing areas. The projection is merely the last stage but one which leads on to the forecast.

A projection is a statistical estimate of the results to be expected in the wider area, calculated from the experimental results and based on a number of assumptions. These assumptions can be summed up as 'all other things being equal', though certain methods of projection take some account of some sources of inequality. Where detailed knowledge of a market has been built up to the extent where a marketing model has been developed, it may be possible to use this to provide a more sophisticated estimate of likely events in the wider market, and this may be called a prediction to distinguish it from the cruder projection.

Whether a projection or a prediction is used to develop the estimate, there will, in most cases, be a number of factors that are known or expected to differ between the experimental areas and the wider market and whose effects will be 'unpredictable' in that no formula can be developed or applied that will efficiently modify the results to take account of them. These factors can therefore only be allowed for as a part of experience and judgement, and it is this process which transforms a projection or prediction into a forecast.

The ideal method of developing a forecast is (a) for the research team to use their specialized knowledge to arrive at the best possible projection, (b) for the marketing team to review the conditions which prevailed in the experimental areas and the conditions expected to prevail in the wider market when the change is made there, and (c) for the two teams together to arrive at the forecast figures. The very least that can emerge from such a dialogue is a better understanding of the problems facing both sides, leading generally to better forecasts and better appreciation of their strengths and limitations.

The types of unpredictable factor which will need to be considered in moving from a projection to a forecast may range over a wide area within the company, outside it in its own market, in the economy generally, or even in the world situation. They may include changes in personnel, technology, competitive strategy, the import situation, or some other aspect of the market. They may reflect specific differences between the conditions of the experiment and the wider application of the change, such as some form of counter-measures by competition, or they may be factors which are affecting or are expected to affect the market more generally. Some that appear as unpredictables at the beginning of the dialogue may be found to be amenable to some form of quantitative assessment through further analysis of the experimental data or of back-data on the wider market.

Methods of projection vary upwards from the very simple, and although the more complex take more factors into account, there can be no guarantee that they will invariably be more accurate. Whichever method is used, and there is much to be said for using more than a single method in any one situation so as to see how the answers are spread, it is always as well to bear in mind that moving directly from an area to a national projection is essentially a short-cut method. It is easier and quicker to project to a single national figure rather than to calculate projections for each major area and then sum them, but where there are marked differences between areas, as in a market with uneven development over a country, the extra effort may be worthwhile. It will at least be illuminating, and if area forecasts are required at a later stage they should anyway be arrived at separately rather than merely being broken down from a national figure.

The main methods of projection are described below. They are described generally as they apply to projecting test-launches, but their application to market testing will be readily apparent.

Projection of brand share

This simply involves taking a recorded brand share of x per cent in the experimental area and projecting the same share on to the wider market. It can be highly fallible as it makes no allowance for any possible variation between the experimental area and the wider market. Quantity estimates are, of course, obtained by applying the projected share to estimates of national market volume. Without this, the projection will form a fairly meaningless statistic.

Another name for this method is projection on a 'buying index basis'. Sales in the experimental area are multiplied by a factor equalling the national sales of the product field divided by the corresponding area sales, thus:

National projection of brand sales

$$= \text{area brand sales} \times \frac{\text{product field national sales}}{\text{product field area sales}}$$

$$= \frac{\text{area brand sales}}{\text{product field area sales}} \times \text{product field national sales}$$

$$= \text{area brand share} \times \text{product field national sales}$$

$$= \text{projection of brand share}$$

Projection of sales per head

Sales of the product per head of population in the experimental area are multiplied by the national population to give an estimate. Among other things, this ignores any possibilities of differential rates of per capita sales between areas, and any attempt to apply a ratio of product group sales nationally as against the test area leads back again to a straight projection of brand share and its application to estimated national product group sales.

Where penetration of the product group is known in the experimental area as well as nationally, a better estimate may be obtained by multiplying sales of the brand per product user in the area by the estimated number of users nationally. For example, if a new gardening product has been tested in the south of England, a projection based on sales per head will lead to an overestimate of the national market because a higher proportion of people have gardens in the south. Projection on the basis of sales per garden owner in the area multiplied by an estimate of the national total of garden owners would give a closer figure.

Projection on purchasing power

In some fields estimates may be available of average regional spending on a group of products or services, such as expenditure on food or motoring. One method of projection is then to calculate the proportion of the appropriate total achieved by the new product in the experimental area and to apply this to the estimated national expenditure in the field; or, alternatively, apply the ratio between national and local expenditure in the field directly to the area sales of the new product. This takes account of possible differences in the numbers actively in the market concerned and of different area rates of expenditure, and this method is often useful when dealing with a product for which there is no 'market' and thus no brand share, as with a new novelty accessory for motorists.

Projection using a known brand

Where a company is already selling one brand in a field and is test-launching another, it should be in a position to produce estimates of sales of the established brand, both in the test area and nationally, which will be more solid than estimates of the total markets. These firmer estimates can be used to provide projections of the sales of the test brand by multiplying the test brand area sales by the national sales of the known brand and dividing by the area sales of the known brand.

$$\text{National projection of new brand} =$$
$$\text{area sales of new brand} \times \frac{\text{national sales of old brand}}{\text{area sales of old brand}}$$

The only benefit given by this method lies in the fact that better estimates will be available of a company's own existing brand than of the market as a whole.

The figures for the old brand included in the equation must, of course, be those which applied before the new brand was introduced into the test area, otherwise, if the old brand has been affected by the new introduction, the ratio will be distorted. If the old brand has not been so affected, the two products may be so different in market appeal as to render this method of dubious merit, as there is an underlying assumption that the two products are sufficiently similar to justify using experience with one to project the other.

Projection by standardizing brand shares

This is a slightly more complex method, developed by the author some years ago and since used with success. (The basic idea is borrowed from the demographers, who use it, among other things, for comparing death-rates among populations with different age structures!)

The method rests on the assumption that differences in consumer attributes, preferences, and behaviour between one area and another will be crystallized in the shares held by existing brands in the market in each area. The calculations then assume that the *proportion* of its sales lost in the test area by each existing brand to the new brand will tend to hold in the wider market. By applying these proportions of test area losses to the existing brand shares of the established products in the wider market, a projection of the likely brand share for the new product is derived.

For example, if Brand X held 40 per cent of the market in the experimental area prior to the test launch, and 30 per cent afterwards, then the proportion of share lost to the new brand is one quarter. If, in the wider market, Brand X has only 28 per cent of the market to start with and loses one quarter of this to the new brand, it will contribute only 7 per cent to the new brand's share. By repeating this calculation for each brand, and for the 'all others' category if necessary, a projection of the new brand share of the wider market can be produced.

Algebraically, if x_0, y_0, etc., are brand shares in the experimental area prior to the introduction of Brand T, and if t_1, x_1, y_1, etc., are the brand shares after the introduction; and if X_0, Y_0, etc., are the brand shares in the wider market prior to the launch, then the projected share of Brand T nationally will be T_1, where

$$T_1 = 100 - \left\{ X_0 \cdot \frac{x_1}{x_0} + Y_0 \cdot \frac{y_1}{y_0} + \ldots \right\}\%$$

This method of 'standardizing' the area share on the national shares calls for more detailed information about the market than do the previous methods, but only for information which should automatically be obtained by anyone undertaking any serious new launch. Even if the formula cannot be used in any particular case, study of it does underline some of the assumptions made in using the simpler methods, such as the need either for virtual equality between x_0 and X_0, y_0 and Y_0, and so on, or for a series of completely compensating differences before the test area market share of t_1 can give a valid direct projection of the national share, T_1.

Projection using segmentation

More refined projections can usually be made if, instead of treating the market as a whole, it is divided into segments in some way. The standardization method above follows this approach, but there are other methods which may be of value, such as looking at the performance of the new product either by type of shop or among consumers in different age groups, social groups, or other classifications.

Results from the test area are used to make separate projections within each group, using one of the methods outlined above, and the projections are brought together by weighting them according to the national pattern. The extent to which the projection differs from one that only uses overall results will depend on the extent to which the segments differ in their behaviour and appear in different proportions in the area as well as nationally. For example, suppose a test-launch has been carried out in an area which has a high proportion of co-operative stores compared with the rest of the country, and has secured a brand share of 19 per cent. Analysis by store type shows that the brand share differs widely between multiples, co-operatives and independents, and that while the three store types in the test area take sales in the product field in the proportions 20 per cent multiples, 50 per cent co-operatives, and 30 per cent through independents, the wider area pattern is 40 per cent multiples, 20 per cent co-operatives, and 40 per cent independents. The following calculation could be made:

Store type	Test area: test brand share in type	Store type share of wider market trade	Contribution to wider brand share
	%	%	%
Multiples	30	40	12·0
Co-operatives	14	20	2·8
Independents	20	40	8·0

Projected brand share: 22·8

The last column of figures is obtained by multiplying the first two together, i.e. the new brand is projected to gain a 30 per cent share of the 40 per cent of product sales through multiples, giving 12 per cent of total sales, etc. The sum of the separate contributions of 22·8 per cent is the projection of the brand share in the wider market.

Whether this will be a better projection of the expected wider market situation will depend on a number of factors, but primarily on whether the differences exhibited between store types in the experimental area are due to store type as such, working through own brands, management attitudes to new products or similar factors, or whether they are merely a reflection of different types of people using different types of store. If it is the former range of factors, then segmentation by store type and re-weighting to the wider market pattern will produce a better projection and the projection of 23 per cent will be better than that of 19 per cent. If it is the latter, and the stores are merely sorting people into types without any particular additional influence on their purchases, then the figure of 23 per cent may not be the better projection and segmentation of the market by consumer types may prove more useful. This is clearly a matter for discussion in any dialogue between those producing the projections and the executives who have experience of the market concerned.

Projection using micro-analytic techniques

Micro-analytic techniques go beyond segmentation, and are concerned with studying the individual behaviour of consumers, their frequency of buying in the field, their loyalty to one brand, their switching between brands, and so forth. As a result, patterns of behaviour may be identified which may be limited to quite small groups of the population, which may, on occasion, defy any other definition than that their purchases follow such a pattern. In some markets, for example, where success or failure may depend on the behaviour of a small group of very heavy users who are not easily identified by ordinary demographic analysis, study of such patterns may be a most fruitful way of establishing precisely what has happened during an experiment and of making projections to a wider market.

Such studies can be of particular use in market testing (or in wider markets) in assessing the effects of promotions or similar activities. The numbers of cases for study, even in a panel of 1,000 households, may be small, so that more powerful methods than those discussed in this book may be needed to test whether observed differences are real or merely within the limits of error, but results can be obtained. In a recent analysis concerning the effects of an offer pack, less than forty people in a panel of 1,000 bought it. The effect on their subsequent rate of purchase of the product was, however, sufficiently marked to show first that a significant increase had occurred, and secondly that the increased sales to the average offer-pack buyer were sufficient to yield additional profits beyond the cost of servicing the coupons redeemed.

Comparisons between methods

The choice of which particular method of projection is used in any given situation will depend on the amount of data available and the complexities of the marketing situation. The method of standardizing brand shares is potentially the most powerful, since it takes more account of inter-area differences than do the others. If wide differences exist between the experimental area and the wider market in, for example, brand shares through shops of different types, segmentation has advantages, and there is no reason why standardization should not be applied within segments if the data is available.

In one by no means atypical set of projections, four different methods of calculation were used and the results were subsequently compared with the performance of the product in the wider market. The comparisons were as shown overleaf.

The dialogue with the marketing team showed that no one would put more faith in any one of the projections based on products A, B, or C than in the others, although, in the event, the projection based on A would have been the most accurate. The projection, based on standard-

Using	Wider market sales
brand share	overestimated by 32%
sales per head	overestimated by 24%
known brand A	overestimated by 4%
known brand B	overestimated by 80%
known brand C	underestimated by 23%
standardization	overestimated by 15%

ization, was the one eventually accepted by the team, and the forecast was reduced to 10 per cent below the projected level to allow for 'unpredictables'. The final gap between the forecast and the result was small – certainly smaller than average for forecasts from test-launches – but this was a first-class experiment, well controlled, adequately measured, and leading on to a most fruitful dialogue.

Where sufficient past data is available about the market concerned, it is always possible to make some prior assessment of the likely efficacy of the alternative methods and to reject those which would be misleading. If the history of a previous launch or change of the type being tested is available, so much the better, even if no specific experiment then preceded introduction into the major market. If, for example, brand shares differ widely by areas, or if sales per head or per user of the product field vary widely, then the simple projections on these bases are unlikely to give a good projection in the new experiment. If, however, standardization of brand share from previous area results to a wider level gave a good projection, the method can be used with greater confidence.

It must be stressed that a previous experiment is not necessary for such assessments to be made. In fact, the most decisive test of the power of a method to give a good projection is whether it can do so from one area to another on a contemporary time basis. The time-lag between an experiment and a wider operation may be a factor which causes a particular projection to appear to be wrong, so if assessments can be made of how the various methods would have behaved during a previous national launch, projecting from single areas to the contemporary national level, only the power of the projection method between areas is involved.

The time-lag

The time-lag between experimental results and the time for which the projection and forecasts are required is often overlooked. The results of the experiment are history, although they may be very recent history, but it may take several months before the wider launch can be mounted, and several more before the effects will be fully developed in the wider market. The projections and forecasts are therefore needed for a situation which may be a year or so in advance of the point at which they are being made. Hence any trends in the market, either in the total level of sales or in movements between brands or in different areas, should be taken into account at the projection stage. For the simpler methods of projection, such as the straight brand share or comparisons with a known brand, the results from the experiment must be set against forecasts of the total market or of the known brand at an appropriate time in the future. Where more complex methods are used, such as standardization of the brand share, the shares of the national market used in the equations should not be those currently observed, but estimates of brand shares in the future based on existing trends or expected developments and timings.

In an experimental launch, the test brand T took share very heavily from brand A, which started with 40 per cent of the market and ended with 15 per cent, and had virtually no effect on brands B and C. While the experiment was running, brands B and C began to take share markedly from brand A in the areas outside the experiment, and A's share fell from 50 to 40 per cent over about four months. Projection from the experimental results, using the standardization method, would have given brand T about 25 per cent of the national market under the conditions of market share prevailing in the wider market at the time when the experiment ended. However, a forecast of the brand shares in the national market a year ahead, by when brand T would have been established, showed that brand A was then expected to be down to only about 20 per cent of the market, with brands B and C gaining share. On this basis, the projection of brand T would only have been about 12 per cent of the market, since there was little evidence from the test that brand T was capable of taking share from brands B or C.

This 12 per cent was not considered to be a sufficient share of the market for a profitable launch, whereas 25 per cent was acceptable, and the problem was whether users of A who had been won over directly by T in the test area could be won in the wider market after they had moved to B or C first. This led to a new series of product placement tests among consumers who had previously used A but were now using B or C, and the results were not encouraging. The decision on whether to go ahead with the new product had now been delayed for about two months, but fortunately the research in the experimental area had been kept up, and it now began to show brand T beginning to lose share to B and C sufficiently for the project to be abandoned.

There are a number of interesting points in this case, but the important one for our purposes is that projections were made not simply for the market situation as it was at the end of the experiment, but as it was expected to be during the future when the product was launched. This was possible because measurements which enabled basic market trends to be observed were being made of the market outside the experimental area. Had spot readings of the wider market alone been available, taken, as often happens, before the beginning of the experiment so that no trend data was available, or had the trends been ignored in making the projection, the projection of a 25 per cent share would almost certainly have led to a decision to proceed. The warning came from a projection based on the forecast trends in competitive brand shares in the wider market.

Market expansion

In happier circumstances, the introduction of a new brand or of more effective methods for marketing an existing product may lead to an expansion of the market itself. This type of movement will normally be identified through comparing experimental results with results from control areas or the rest of the wider market, and account should be taken of such movements in making projections.

These movements may contain two elements in differing proportions: (a) expansion specifically due to the new product attracting new users to itself from outside the previously existing market among people who had not previously, or not at least recently, bought the existing products; or (b) a more general expansion shared with the other brands on the market which are also attracting new users. In the first case, the new product can be considered as having opened up a sub-market of its own, as may happen when some new appeal has been developed. The second case is often found when a third or fourth brand is introduced as a 'me-too' into a developing market which has out-run the initial impetus of the first introductions and which triggers off the next phase of expansion.

Identification of precisely what has happened to cause expansion, and whether it is specific or general, will call for detailed examination of buying patterns from consumer diaries, or it may possibly be obtainable from the results of consumer surveys. In projecting from the experimental to the wider area, it is technically possible to treat the two components separately and to project them by different methods, but generally the differences are marginal between such projections and those in which the expansion of the experimental market is applied as a growth factor to the wider market. What is important is that, if there is a large specific element in the expansion, the factors on which this depended, and which should be taken into account in projection, are often unknown; or even if they can be identified and quantified in the experimental area, their importance in the wider market may be unknown. Hence the overall projection may be somewhat less robust than is the case with a static market.

Consider an extreme case where the expansion of a market has been wholly specific and where only the experimental brand has gained users from outside the existing market. For each 100 units previously sold by the existing brands, sales with the new product in the market rise to 120, of which the new product takes fifty. Of these sales of fifty, thirty can be traced to existing users of the product and twenty to new users on some acceptable definition, showing that the market expansion is specific to the new product. There are then three ways of proceeding:

1 To project on the basis that the new product has captured 50/120, or 42 per cent of a market that has expanded by 20 per cent.
2 To project on the basis that the new product has captured 30 per cent of the existing market, and will add the expected total market expansion to its sales.
3 To project on the basis that the new product has captured 30 per cent of the existing market, and that for every thirty items sold in the wider market to existing users, it will sell twenty to new users.

The first method assumes that the measured expansion in the experimental market can be applied directly to the wider market, although the 42 per cent share may be modified, depending on the method of projection used. Since the expansion rate may be highly dependent on the impact of the new product, it may be unwise to use this method if the projected market share differs markedly from the experimental result.

The second method separates the two factors and allows for projection to the wider level on the basis of the 30 per cent share of the existing market, with such modification of the expansion factor as may seem appropriate from analysis of the sectors in the experimental area in which it occurred and knowledge of the demographic composition of, or other factors in, the wider market.

The third method uses the observed ratio from the experimental area between sales gained from existing users and those gained from new users. This will generally be a better guide where the projected market share differs widely from that observed in the experiment, and it still permits the application of any other relevant factors in moving from the projection to a forecast.

The same arguments apply to the results of market testing, where changes in the campaign, advertising pressure, price, packaging, or other factors may lead to expansion of the market with or without attracting users of other existing brands.

In all cases where a marked expansion occurs, the experimental change may, to some extent, have opened up a new market that may differ to a greater or lesser extent from the old one, and inevitably that part of the projections concerned with this new element is likely to be less firmly based than the part based on the old market. The underlying assumptions are extended to cover the existence of untapped potential in other areas in line with that found in the experimental area; of similar propensities among those not even using the type of product to come into the market for the new brand; and so forth. The strength of these assumptions needs examination in every case where there is marked expansion, and the projections need reviewing in the light of any weaknesses.

The precision of projections

The precision of any projection, whether or not involving market expansion, depends on the accuracy of the research results from the experimental area and on the validity of the methods of projection used. In experiments in the laboratory or in field trials, limits of error can be placed on projections of results, but in marketing this is seldom possible, either because the experiment is conducted in too few areas for any valid assessment to be made of the variability of the results, or else because, even where more than a single area is used, they are seldom selected at random and the basis for such calculations is destroyed.

The possible range of error in a projection will be some function of the standard error and a projection error, and will be such that it cannot be less than either. Thus research which starts with 95 per cent limits of error of $\pm$ 10 per cent cannot lead to a projection with any narrower limits than this. If the method of projection is 100 per cent efficient, including efficiency in projecting forward through time where this is required, then the precision of the projection will be the same as for the research results. The efficiency of different methods can sometimes be assessed retrospectively by examining past data from the market, and more faith can be put into a method which would have worked well in the past, but while such an examination should lead to the rejection of methods which would have failed in the market, there can be no immediate guarantee that the remainder will work in the future.

If the examination of a market and the factors affecting it has been taken to the stage where a model can be produced, two benefits immediately follow. The first is that it should be possible to determine from the model, and in advance of the experiment, the results likely to be obtained under the conditions existing in the experimental area. This greatly facilitates the optimum allocation of research resources for making measurements of the most relevant factors to indicate both intermediate and ultimate changes in the system. Secondly, the observed results can be compared with these expectations. If the results are as expected, then they can be taken as confirmation that the model is capable of predicting the outcome of the application of the experimental changes in the wider market, having succeeded in doing this in the experimental area. If the expectations are not confirmed, then further analysis will indicate where the deviations from expectation have occurred, such as in establishing the distribution or the awareness of a new product, and this information can be fed into the model to yield an appropriately modified wider market projection. For the great majority of companies and markets, however, models possessing the required degree of sophistication do not as yet exist.

Forecasting

Projection is fallible, and the results need to be assessed, modified, or even recalculated in the light of knowledge and experience of the market, as it has been, as it is, and as it is expected to be. This is the development of the forecast, and it is the last essential stage in the conduct and interpretation of an experiment. The factors which need to be considered will vary from one market to another, and from one time to another. For example, at the present time in Great Britain (1970), the effects of decimalizing the currency will need to be considered. Nothing so far known, or foreseeable, will enable the possible effects of currency changes to be quantified and built into any system of projection, and any likely effects of decimalization on a product must be allowed for at the stage of forecasting.

While forecasting cannot be carried out to a set of rules, it is useful, and sometimes salutary, to start the exercise with a full review of the history of the experiment under four headings:

1 Was the experiment intended to produce projectable results? If it was planned, controlled, and measured for this purpose, well and

good. But if it was originally undertaken as a less rigorous experiment, such as merely checking the comprehension of the advertising, and sales data have been obtained as a by-product, then the projections should be treated with some reserve.

2 Was the integrity of the experiment maintained, or were there areas, internal or external, where experimental discipline broke down ? Was any action taken at any time, even from the best of motives, that would not be reproducible on a wider scale, and that might have affected the results? In some experiments, owing sometimes to bad planning, sometimes to an unexpectedly favourable response, shortage of supplies has placed an artificial ceiling on the level of sales achieved, with obvious effects on the results and projections. Numerous things may have happened to impair the integrity of the experiment and which may call for consideration when developing a forecast.

3 Was the experiment run for long enough to allow the full effects to develop? Are the latest results obtained stable, or are there still signs of movement, upwards or downwards, which need to be considered? Premature termination of experiments is probably a major cause of misleading projections, and where problems of timing lead to such situations, allowance must as far as possible be made in the forecast.

4 What was measured in the experiment? Definitions are vital. Seldom is it possible to measure sales of a product to all consumers and there will normally be some limitations, as when sales are measured through stores of given types or to consumers in given categories. Some part of sales will go through other types of store, or to other types of consumer, and allowance must be made, sometimes in projection but frequently in forecasting, for these unmeasured sectors.

Given sound research and the proper combination of statistical and marketing expertise in developing projections and forecasts, there is no reason why adequate estimates of the likely outcome of launches or other marketing changes should not be made. There is, however, an urgent need to keep the forecasts under continuous review, both before and after the wider market operation is undertaken. The likely effects of any changes in the market generally, or any subsequent deviations from the expected lines of development, should be followed through to a reappraisal of the forecast if necessary. This may be greatly facilitated, and a great deal of time saved, if the processes and considerations which led up to the original forecast and to any subsequent amendments are properly documented.

The drop factor

The results obtained in the wider market should be constantly compared with those in the experimental area, so that an early warning of deviations is obtained. Apart from this, there is one particular statistic which appears to be worthy of consideration: the 'drop factor'.

Figure 10.1

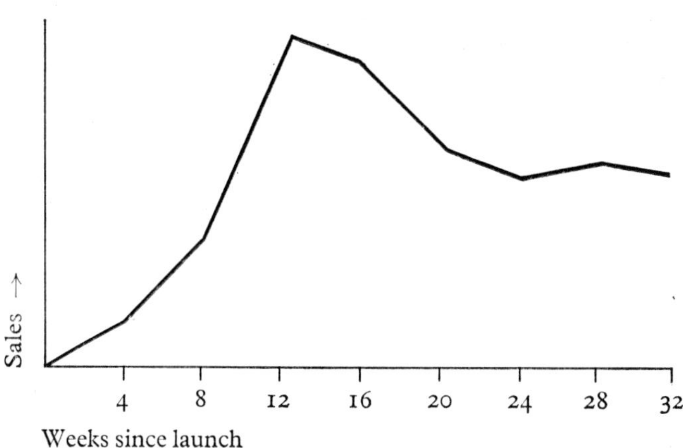

The typical pattern of retail sales of a new product is shown in Figure 10.1, with an initial rise in sales to a peak, followed by a decline to a plateau that is often raised again by the second wave of promotional activity. The 'drop factor' (D) is merely the percentage fall from the peak level of sales to the plateau or stable level, i.e.:

$$D = \frac{\text{peak sales} - \text{stable level}}{\text{peak sales}} \times 100$$

Analysis of a number of packaged products shows that the average drop is of the order of 40 per cent, but the scatter about this average is too wide for the figure to be of any use in making forward estimates from the peak to the stable level. Neither has any relationship been found between the shape of the curve during the build-up to the peak and the shape of the declining part. Some products build up quickly and fall slowly, some build up slowly and fall quickly, so that extrapolation of the stable level from the sales curve is itself not possible, although, as explained in Chapter 9, extrapolation of the brand share is possible from analysis of penetration and repeat-purchasing patterns.

The value of the drop factor lies in an apparent tendency for it to remain roughly constant from the experimental market to the wider market, or through successive areas of a rolling launch. Thus, if in an experimental launch the drop factor has been found to be x per cent, then once the sales line has been seen to turn over in the wider launch, an estimate of the likely stable level can be obtained by applying the factor to the observed peak level. This has been shown to operate not only when the two peak levels are similar, but also when they are widely different. Figure 10.2 shows the application of the drop factor, calculated from the first area in a rolling launch and applied to subsequent areas where for a variety of reasons the product achieved markedly different sales levels.

Figure 10.2 Application of the drop factor

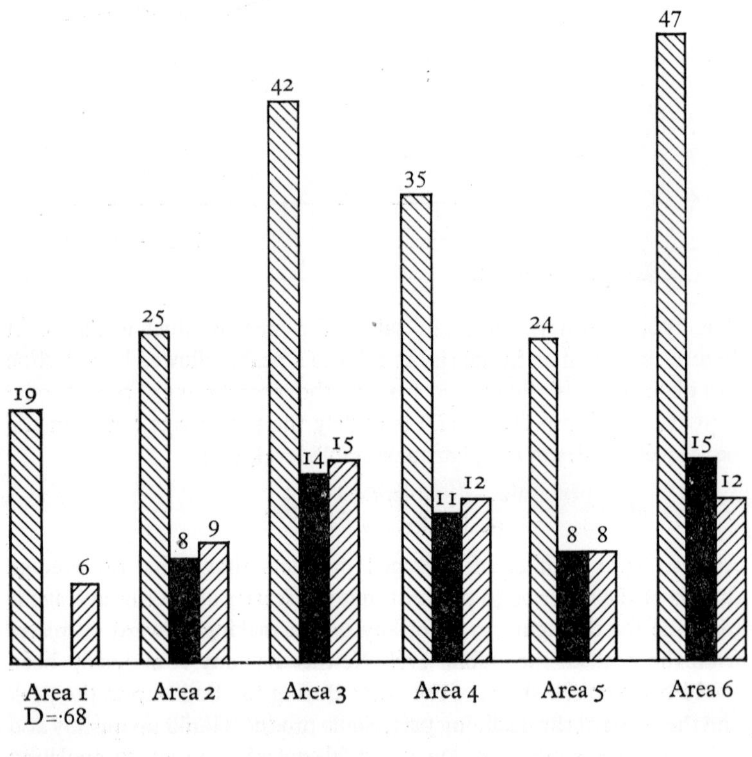

The drop factor is highly dependent on the interval between successive readings of the sales figures, since the longer the intervals the less pronounced the pattern will appear. If, therefore, the experiment has been measured at monthly intervals, the factor obtained will not apply directly to measurements of a wider operation measured at two-monthly intervals; recalculation is needed by grouping the monthly readings in pairs.

To sum up, projection and forecasting depend at this stage partly on science but largely on experience and art. Greater understanding of markets, both in general and for particular products, leading to the development of better means of projection and ultimately to practical marketing models, will increase the scientific contribution. But the art will still remain, concentrated on the true intangibles of the situation instead of being dissipated, as now, in making allowances for gaps and shortcomings in the scientific contribution.

11

Some practical problems

Problems arise at every stage in marketing experiments, and will vary from one market to another as well as from one situation to another within a market. They tend to become more complex, and their proper solution more important, as one moves from simple feasibility or pilot operations to projectable launches of new products, and the success of any experiment will depend largely on the skill with which problems are diagnosed and handled.

One major source of trouble in the interpretation and projection of results is that problems may not have been recognized during the earlier stages of planning and execution. Most of these can be recognized and avoided if sufficient thought is given at the planning stage and critical comparisons made between what is being put into the experimental area and what will eventually be put into the wider market. Provided it is done, this will often reveal that certain subsidiary factors have been overlooked which could possibly either wreck the experiment completely or else cast considerable doubt on the validity of any results obtained.

Subsidiary factors

Such oversights often occur when comparatively simple experiments on a single aspect of an existing marketing mix are made and the possible consequences not fully thought through. This happened, in different ways, in two pressure tests, both of which were planned in the belief that a considerable increase in advertising effort would help to open up the market, and where the experimental levels of the appropriation were to be well above the current level.

In the first example, the pressure test was to be run in three areas at, respectively, double, three times, and four times the current level, continuing with the development of a campaign that had already been proved. A factor overlooked until quite late in the planning, though caught in time for action to be taken, was the relationship existing between the level of the appropriation (being spent wholly on television) and the number of commercials to be used during the year. The national campaign, running at the normal level, was to be covered by six different commercials, and these six were also to be used in the experimental areas. The unrecognized factor was the question of whether six commercials were adequate, particularly in the area that was to receive four times the existing weight of advertising. This was a difficult question to answer, since little is known of the 'wear-out' effects on commercials, but two conclusions were reached. First, it was generally agreed that if the higher levels of appropriation should ever be adopted nationally, the number of commercials used would certainly be increased, though not necessarily *pro rata*; secondly, it was agreed that to run tests on the two top levels of appropriation with only six commercials would not provide a valid indication of what might subsequently be achieved nationally.

Recognition of the problem led to a proper formulation of the numbers of commercials which would probably be used if the three experimental appropriations were to be used nationally. The production costs involved in making the full number of commercials required for the four-times test were thought not to be justified at that stage, but some additional money was budgeted to increase the number available above six. This partly solved the problem, and the remainder was overcome, at least to the satisfaction of the group, through two compromises. The first was to re-use some earlier commercials from the same campaign which could be slotted in with the new material; this increased the number of commercials sufficiently to meet the requirements of the double and treble appropriation areas over a full year. The second was to run the four-times area for nine months, making full and logical use of the available commercials, and to complete the year using re-runs. The alternative was to terminate this four-times test after nine months and to judge its effect at that stage, but it was thought that there might be cumulative effects that should be given a proper chance to develop and which would not be unduly affected by re-running commercials already used.

Technically some problem areas remained in the adopted compromise solution, notably that there could be no guarantee of whether the additional commercials would be more or less effective than the original six. This could have been solved by screening, in those parts of the rest of the country being used as a control, various combinations of six commercials from among the original six and from the additional ones used in the test. This, however, would have added to the complexity of the operation, and it was diplomatically decided not to pursue the matter, but to be content with the major improvement already achieved in the experiment.

The second example of a pressure test that was planned without proper regard to related factors was a simpler operation involving a doubling of appropriation in a single television area, conveniently covered by a single depot. As happens sometimes, the company research manager was only brought into the discussion at a late stage when requested to organize ways of measuring the results. He immediately asked how large an increase in sales was expected, and was told that no specific figure had been set, but that the experiment was merely to find out what would happen. The research manager therefore rephrased his question and asked how large an increase in sales would be needed to cover the increased expenditure on advertising. This, again, had not been calculated, so as he needed some figures from which to work out how precise the research measurements would need to be to be useful, he calculated his own figure from internal cost data.

The research manager reported back with a recommendation, based on his calculations, that an increase in sales of x per cent would be needed to cover the additional appropriation. The figure of x per cent was accepted as reasonable and the recommendation approved. Some days later it was realized that the depot concerned could not cope with an increase in trade of x per cent, neither was it possible to make other immediate arrangements to cope with such an increase. The experiment was therefore transferred to another area which was less satisfactory in some ways, but where at least any rise in sales could develop unhampered by restrictions on supply.

The problems in these two cases were overcome comparatively easily once they had been uncovered. But the hazards arose in the first place because of attention being so closely focused on the main objectives of the experiments that other factors were left out of consideration. Other types of problem are more easily identified, but may be less amenable to solution, as when some slight differences may occur between a product made in a pilot plant for an experimental launch and the product as it will eventually come off the main production line. Here possibly nothing can be done until the forecasting stage, when some allowance may be made for the effects of such a difference.

Advertising schedules

Scaling down a press campaign from a national level to a small area presents problems in most countries, especially if magazines are to be used for which no local equivalents exist. In Great Britain, the situation has been eased to some extent by the increasing availability of split-run facilities in the national daily press and the introduction of 'tipping-in' facilities in some magazines. These do not, however, solve the problem completely, partly because a proposed national schedule is seldom completely covered by the facilities and partly because of boundary conditions.

Three main methods are generally possible in scaling a press campaign down to a small area: (a) the direct scaling down of the appropriation on a population basis; (b) the purchase of similar numbers of insertions of appropriate sizes; or (c) the purchase of a schedule designed to match the proposed national schedule in terms of reach and frequency. Of these, the third is probably the most generally acceptable, but there may be difficulties in obtaining comparable data and there is the more abstruse problem of comparative effectiveness of local as against national media. Judgement on what sort of schedule, or even which types of media, will best approximate to a proposed national campaign is very often of far greater importance than mere statistical comparability.

In contrast, the problems of using television in a small area appear to be far more simple, involving only the application of the proposed national schedule to a local station. There are, however, a number of problems, some of which are clearly shared with the press media, though for the sake of simplicity they are discussed here solely in terms of television.

Four main types of experimental situation tend to occur so far as time-buying is concerned; three are concerned with experiments relating to existing products, where an aspect of the marketing mix is to be varied, and the fourth is concerned with test launching a new product. The four types of situation are:

1 Experiments concerned with existing products in which the weight of advertising is not the subject of the test, as in experiments on a new campaign, changed prices, a new pack, etc. Here the media objective must be to get as near as possible to the received pattern of advertising in previous periods among the target group, irrespective of cost, otherwise any major changes in the received pattern of impacts or opportunities-to-see may vitiate the test.

2 Experiments on existing products in which the appropriation in an area is to be varied by agreed proportions, e.g. up 50 per cent, or down 30 per cent, to assess the effects of changes in appropriation levels. Here the buyer's objective should be to spend the revised appropriation as efficiently as possible within his general brief, but

experiments should not normally be put into areas where card-rate structures or proneness to deals would produce highly atypical changes in schedules. If, for example, a 50 per cent increase in appropriation could be expected to yield, say, a 60 per cent increase in spots or rating points, areas which would yield considerably larger increases should not be used. When, for some reason, their use is unavoidable, then it would seem preferable to buy in that area the type of schedule which the change in the appropriation would normally permit in a more typical area; and to buy in the test area irrespective of cost.

3 Experiments in which other aspects, including the appropriation, are to be held at their former levels, but where the structure of the schedule is the subject of the experiment, as in assessing the effects of burst *versus* continuous advertising, or of different types or lengths of spot. This would normally mean that the existing appropriation should be spent to the best possible advantage within the brief covering the new schedule. The same qualifications about ab-normalities in any particular area would apply here, as in (2) above.

4 Experimental launches in which the proposed national television advertising is to be introduced into an area. This raises a number of problems, some specific to television, and some common to other forms of media as well.

Not infrequently there may be two possible patterns of advertising that could be set up in an experimental launch area: either a replica of a proposed national pattern or else the specific pattern which an area would receive if it were itself part of a national launch. Whether, in practice, there is any difference in scale between the two will depend on the way in which the company intends to break down the national appropriation for the new product by areas. In so far as an experiment is normally designed to reproduce national conditions on a small scale, then the national pattern should be put into the experimental area, but there may well be instances where the other is more appropriate.

Even putting in the national pattern may form a compromise, since a national pattern may not exist except in so far as it is an 'average' of differing area patterns. However, assuming it is to be put in, then it is possible to specify this national pattern in a number of ways, such as the size of the appropriation, the schedule (i.e. the numbers, lengths, and timings of spots during a period), the cumulative sum of ratings achieved by the schedule, or in more complex terms involving reach and frequency.

Specifying the area appropriation as a fraction of the proposed national figure puts the real weight of advertising in the experimental area at the mercy of the rate-card, and this may lead to marked differences between areas in what is transmitted. Since these differences are often quite arbitrary – at least so far as the experiment is concerned – specifications in terms of appropriations should not normally be used.

Specifying the numbers of spots of different lengths and their timings over a period involves transforming the national appropriation into a schedule, then buying this schedule in the experimental area, regardless of costs or whether they are above or below the *pro rata* level. In this way the experimental area is subjected to a 'national' schedule, assuming that it exists. However, local variations in viewing habits may lead to more or fewer opportunities to see the schedule than would be the case if it was in fact being used nationally. This leads us to the idea that what is required in the area is not a particular pattern of transmissions, but the establishment of an appropriate pattern of reception among the target audience.

To meet this requirement, it will be necessary to transform the national appropriation into some measure of the reception of the commercials; cumulated rating points are the simplest form, but even these raise two further problems. First, the methods of measuring ratings currently in use depend on comparatively small samples, particularly in the smaller television areas most frequently used for experiments, so that sampling errors attached to the absolute levels of ratings may be quite wide. Suppose, for example, that area ratings of 30 per cent are observed when the national level is 25 per cent. If the area panel is less than about 200 homes, this difference could merely be due to sampling error, or it may indicate a real difference. If it is real, then the cumulative rating required can be built up in the experimental area with only five sixths of the number of spots required on a national basis; but if the observed difference is only sampling error, then the full number of spots will be required. This problem can sometimes be resolved by considering such other data apart from the rating panels as surveys in which some aspect of viewing habits has been covered. These data are likely to be less specific than the ratings, but comparisons between areas will indicate whether any of the differences shown by panels are reflected in other research, and how they should be interpreted. Panel results will, of course, give very precise measurements of the relative audience to spots within an area.

The second problem is that, if differences exist between area ratings, so that equalization of cumulative ratings leads to different numbers of spots per period, then the pattern of exposure for individuals will be affected. If frequency of viewing the campaign is – or even could be – a factor in response, the experimental situation could again begin to vary from the national pattern it is meant to represent.

It seems then that the specification of the advertising effort to be put into an experimental launch needs to be made in terms of reach and frequency among the target group, if the buyer is to be reasonably certain of establishing the required national replica. Thus, the proposed national appropriation should first be turned into a form of reach and frequency matrix, a schedule for the experimental area then being constructed to meet this matrix. Since, however, it will in many cases be possible to meet this requirement with any one of a number of schedules, any choice between them should be exercised so as to select that schedule which departs least from the likely national schedule. Unfortunately, the above comments about the sampling errors in the panel ratings will apply even more forcibly to frequency schedules, and judgement is needed if the buyer is to avoid a disproportionate effort being made to accommodate apparent differences between national and area patterns which are not true reflections of differences between the populations concerned.

Relationship to competitive advertising

So far this problem of devising appropriate schedules for an experimental launch has been considered as if the new product was entering a fresh field and encountering no competitive activity. In practice, three different situations calling for different treatments may be encountered.

The first is where a product is entering an existing market in which competitive advertising effort is fairly uniform between areas. Here the average national pattern, defined in terms of reach and frequency or other methods, can usually be applied in the experimental area, and will provide a reasonable balance between the weights of advertising for the new product and its competitors.

The second is where the market is one in which existing competitive advertising shows marked differences between areas, but all brands follow the same general pattern. Here the problem is slightly more complex. If the schedule for the new product is based on the national average, then the relationship between it and the competitive advertising efforts in the area may not be typical and doubt may be thrown on the validity of the results. The alternative is to put in an area schedule which will produce a proper balance between the new product advertising and competition, but, clearly, in re-establishing this relationship the reach and frequency may become to some extent removed from the proposed national pattern.

The third situation is more complex still and arises when competitors are following different policies in their area allocations of the appropriation, with the result that their respective efforts vary from area to area. Hence it becomes unlikely that either relative or absolute levels of competitive advertising will be typical in the experimental area. The ideal way out of this difficulty is to experiment in more than one area and to select a number of areas including various forms of atypicality, so that together the areas will approximate to the national pattern. This is, however, unlikely to prove possible in practice, either because of the costs and risks involved in a larger experiment or because of administrative difficulties in running a multi-area experimental launch.

The inevitable conclusion is that each case must be considered on its merits. In those instances where a simple structure of competitive advertising exists, or even where no competitive advertising at all, there will be simple answers. In more complex cases it will be necessary to consider the type of market and the comparative importance to be attached to achieving relative levels against competition or to achieving required levels of reach and frequency. If relative levels against competition cannot all be met at the same time, then decisions must be taken in the light of the importance of various existing brands to the launch and matching arranged accordingly.

The problems of deciding on the appropriate pattern of advertising for an experimental launch have been dealt with at some length because it has often been said that scaling down a television appropriation to an experimental area is quite simple. And it is true to say that, when compared with some of the problems that may arise in other directions, it has the advantage of the medium remaining the same, though the problem of securing an appropriate schedule to meet the purposes of the experiment can still present difficulties.

One difficulty that occurs in marketing experiments where changes in media or campaigns are being tested, is that of digging holes in the existing schedules, whether press or electronic, to accommodate test advertising. In Great Britain, testing a change from press to television advertising tends to be difficult, since existing press advertising must be withdrawn from the television area first, and even with the increasing numbers of regional editions this still presents problems when national newspapers and magazines are involved. In the United States, similar problems occur when it is necessary to dig a hole in network television, though usually this can be organized at a price.

Distribution problems

Some of the problems associated with gaining distribution for a new product, such as avoiding too deep or too personal an involvement from the sales force, or too many visitors from outside, were mentioned in Chapter 2. This type of problem is solved by eternal vigilance, but there are other problems which call for specific decisions. Often, for example, a new product will during a national launch have the benefit of trade advertising which is denied to it during an experimental launch. Further, the experimental results are often quoted during the wider launch, either in trade advertising or in direct mail shots, brochures, or other means. Logically, if these items are deemed to be worth expenditure during the national launch, then their absence from the test-launch may lead to lower levels of distribution or some other weakness in the initial impact of the product. This raises the problem of what, if anything, should be done to remedy the situation, and many companies feel justified in using some of the supplementary services offered by media owners, such as reception facilities, exhibitions and displays, point-of-sale material linking the product with the medium, teams of representatives, and so forth. Undoubtedly there are occasions when for a new product a cold sell would make slower progress in a test launch than it would be expected to achieve on a wider market backed by successful test results and trade advertising and promotion; the substitution of other means of approaching the trade is then justified. The problem remains that there is no easy way of assessing what combination of activities will justly compensate for those not available in the test, and here the judgement of executives is the only guide (care being taken to avoid over-compensation leading to unduly optimistic results).

Distribution can often suffer from the unwillingness of some major multiple organizations to take products which are only available in limited test areas, despite representations at high levels. If the number of stores affected is small, and there are numbers of other similar outlets in the area, the damage done may be slight and may be compensated for at the forecasting stage, but if the organizations concerned are strong in the area, the gap in the data may be too serious to be compensated for adequately in this way, and the validity of the results as a whole may become doubtful. Clearly this type of problem is best avoided by checking in an area before becoming committed to using it, but if it is unavoidable, some relief may be obtained through segmentation of the results. With consumer panels, it may be possible to analyse separately first those consumers who appear not to visit the stores in question but who confine their purchasing to other sectors; secondly, those who use those stores as well as others; and finally, those who only shop at the stores concerned. Then, assuming that the first group will not have been affected by the decision not to stock the test product, the performance in this sector of the market can be evaluated directly. In the second group, partial evaluation is achieved and a projection may be possible to assumed levels of full distribution. In the third group, a largely subjective assessment, aided by any indications from the behaviour of the other two groups, may be all that is possible.

With store-panel data, similar analyses may be practicable, first by store type, taking out the independents and assuming they will not have been affected, then co-operatives, then the stocking multiples, and finally the non-stockists on policy grounds. The total pattern is then rebuilt from the pieces.

Whether it is consumer panel or store panel data which are used, the methods remain a makeshift, and must inevitably contain dubious assumptions about the behaviour of consumers or stores when the new product is lacking from one part of the distributive system; no amount of calculation or manipulation at the forecasting stage can guarantee to cover this eventuality.

Conversely, a problem may occur where a retail or wholesale organization in the experimental area is willing to take the product but unwilling or unable to limit its distribution to the specific area of the test. This problem is increasing with the development of cash-and-carry wholesale warehouses, but from the experimental point of view, apart from affecting measurements based on the analysis of factory sales, this does not generally matter, since any effects will develop outside the test area and should not affect the results there. In some cases, it is anyway of small consequence if the spillage is merely going into an area where no other commercial interests are involved. In others, however, such spillage into areas in which other important customers of the company are operating may have serious political and commercial repercussions. This may at least lead to friction and misunderstanding, and possibly even to a loss of trade for existing products or to the rapid extension of the experimental marketing area if other wholesale or retail organizations relax or abandon restrictions on distribution. The resolution of these problems, through the use of other areas if necessary, is essential before any test operation is launched.

Comparisons of research results

One frequent problem which arises in the assessment of results, whether of test launching or of market testing, is that research measurements of different types may appear to indicate different results. This applies particularly to measures of sales where comparisons can be made between the results of sales analysis, store audits, and consumer panels.

The first point to check in such cases is the definition of the measure of sales being recorded, since the three measures will almost certainly be differently based. Fluctuations in wholesale or warehouse stocks, including the initial filling of the pipeline, will lead to differences between factory sales and the deliveries recorded by store panels. If, as is generally the case, the store panel covers only certain specified types of outlet, such as food stores, this again may give rise to differences, not only when compared with factory sales, but also when compared with purchases by a consumer panel. This last will record purchases from the full range of stores, but will exclude purchases made by offices, stores, boarding-houses, hotels, and other institutions, whether made at wholesale or retail level. Thus there are often good reasons for differences in the measurements obtained, and proper examination can often provide useful information (see Figure 1.1).

A second cause of differences, particularly early on in the course of an experiment, is one of timing, either because of lags in the system as supplies travel down the pipeline, or because different measurements are made on different time scales. Comparisons between monthly sales analyses and bi-monthly or four-weekly research panels operating on a variety of dates can call for a certain amount of rearrangement of data before the various parts can be properly fitted together.

Also to be taken into account is the fact that each research measurement is unavoidably subject to some degree of sampling error. Assuming that each research operation was properly vetted before commission, and that it has been carried out by a reputable company, then if in the final analysis discrepancies still appear between figures, the values can be placed in a simple model of the situation and assessments made of the flow of goods so as to give the greatest weight at each stage to the most direct measurement, but without disregarding evidence at other levels.

The key to most of the problems in experimental marketing lies in adequate and early analysis of a whole project, its objective, the means to carry it through, and the options between which a choice will finally be made. To do this demands knowledge, experience, and time. Senior

Figure 11·1

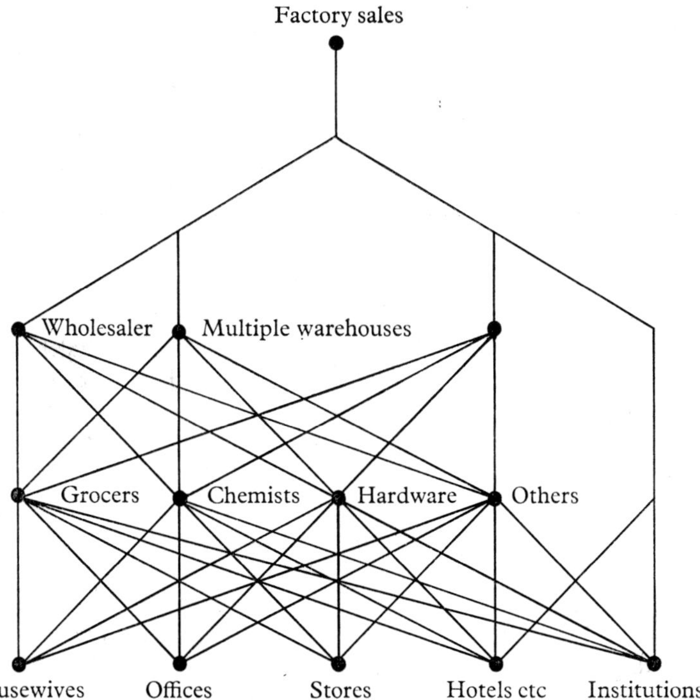

management will possess the first two attributes, but frequently lack the third, and in many cases its involvement regrettably tends to be somewhat intermittent or localized on particular aspects. The virtual ability to ring up a media owner and 'buy' a six months' test operation 'off the peg' has meant that management can be saved a great deal of detailed planning in this particular respect, but while this is a valuable facility, it should not be allowed to obscure the need for very careful analysis of other problem areas at a high level if mistakes are to be avoided and valid results obtained.

12

Areas for further development

At the beginning of this book it was indicated that marketing experiments are basically concerned with three types of variable: the independent, the dependent, and the exogenous. The independent variables are those that are to be varied or changed for the experiment, such as advertising pressure or content, pack, price, use of promotions, etc. The dependent variable is generally some measure of sales, since normally the ultimate objective of marketing activity is to affect profits through sales, though more immediate results of a change in the marketing mix, such as a shift in awareness or a change of image, may become the dependent variable. The exogenous variables are those not of immediate concern in the experiment but which may have some influence on the results to be measured over which there is no control, like competitive advertising or the weather, or those other factors in one's own marketing mix that can and should be controlled during the course of an experiment.

Developments affecting the independent variables are at least partly under the control of companies engaged in experiments, and may take the form of operating more ambitious experimental programmes, such as seeking an optimum appropriation level through a series of experiments rather than merely testing one or two possible alternatives to a current level. Other developments, possibly generated by media owners or research organizations, will affect the ease with which the independent variables can be manipulated, largely by reducing the minimum area required for experimental purposes. In Great Britain, these developments may include more regional facilities in the press and split-runs or some form of 'tipping-in' or other inserts; and, in television, the possibility of using some UHF transmitters independently of the remainder of the network for experimental purposes.

The behaviour in experiments of the dependent variable is normally assessed through measurements obtained from samples of people or stores that are then subjected to a form of statistical analysis. Methods of sampling are unlikely to change in themselves, though there may be further refinements in stratification, and the use of computers in analysis enables more complex systems of weighting to be used with ease. Neither of these refinements, however, is likely to make a startling difference to the situation.

There is more scope for development in practice through the use of more powerful methods of experimental design and statistical analysis but this will only become possible if the marketing companies are able and willing to finance, organize, and control multi-area experiments as opposed to the current preponderance of single area tests. The statistical techniques are already there, and have been there for years. In many cases, the facilities already exist, even if making full use of them does call for some such effort as digging holes in the existing media pattern. In Great Britain, one problem in the past, though not an insuperable one, has been the pattern of television advertising, with its limited number of transmitters, these often serving areas unacceptable in particular experiments because of size, location, or other factors. It remains to be seen whether the new, more numerous, and more localized UHF stations will offer advantages in this direction, or whether they will remain firmly embedded in their networks.

More detailed analysis of data

Increased use will in the future be made of the data collected, in particular from panels of consumers or stores, so as to provide information beyond the averages or percentages at which most analysis now tends to stop. Already an increasing use can be seen of more detailed analyses of brand-switching patterns to show which consumers have moved from one product to another and which have remained 'loyal'. Interpreting these patterns depends on having some knowledge of what is normal in a market, so that *real* changes can be distinguished from the continuous changes always present even under the most static of average rates of purchasing or brand shares. At the consumer end of the market, for frequently purchased products at least, a great deal of attention has in recent years been focused on these switching and loyalty patterns, and although there is considerable, and even acrimonious, discussion as to which of a number of possible mathematical systems best describes the real situation, even at an empirical level sufficient knowledge exists for these to be useful in interpreting experimental results.

Two areas which have so far received comparatively little attention are the patterns of sales of consumer goods out of retail stores and the patterns of purchases of consumer durables. Some work has been done, and as is so often the case in marketing, more has certainly been done than has yet been published. A number of research companies are looking into the data in efforts to provide for more effective interpretation of the movements that certainly lie beneath changes in the averages, and that probably also exist beneath unchanging average conditions.

While much of the research into these and other relevant patterns must come from research companies, universities and business schools, or research foundations, individual companies could in general do far more to collect and codify information within their own organizations than they do at present. Few, however, can hope to go as far as the American company which was able to display to the author the launch sales patterns of fourteen products in the same field, all launched during Augusts over the previous few years. Nevertheless, the systematic collection and appraisal of data relating to past changes in a market, whether in experiments or on a full-scale level, may reveal significant differences in pattern between those that eventually became successful and those that failed. Even knowing that no identifiable pattern exists is useful and may prevent a premature decision being reached in a later operation.

Where such studies lead to the development of a model of a market from which predictions can be made of the likely effect on the dependent variable of changing the independent variables, then marketing experiments can be framed far more specifically and measurements geared more directly to recording changes in expected dimensions. The experiments can then be used to confirm, or reject, the predictions obtained from the model, with the probable result that fewer experiments will be needed, thus releasing resources for the remaining ones concerned with vital issues.

The development of models, even early conceptual models in advance of more detailed mathematical models, will focus attention on the interactions between the different parts of the marketing mix. At present, most marketing experiments, other than launches, are concerned with the effects of changing a single variable, such as an appropriation, a price, a campaign or some other factor. In many cases this is justifiable, as when a new campaign is being tested. In others, however, it can lead to a wrong reading of the real situation, as when two or more factors interact strongly, so that moving either of them separately will lead to a marginal change in sales while varying both together may lead to marked changes. For example, it may be quite possible that increasing the distribution of a product in isolation may, if there has been no reservoir of unrequited demand, give no benefit in consumer purchases. Similarly, increased advertising may not change the sales pattern of a product if it is not widely available. Changing both situations together may lead to a result far in excess of what either change on its own was capable of producing. Clearly separate experiments on distribution or advertising could lead to a conclusion that no benefit would be derived from either course, the existence of interaction between them only being determinable through an experiment combining changes in both at the same time.

Looking for interactions on an empirical basis is likely to prove costly. If there are, say, eight variable factors in a marketing mix over which the company has control, and which are therefore eligible as independent variables in experiments, there exist a potential twenty-eight interactions between pairs of factors; and there may well be more between triads and larger multiples. Some of these can probably be dismissed as unlikely, but the number remaining which could possibly affect the profitability of a product could well exceed experimental capacity. The value of a model based on past measurements and changes is that it will enable the important interactions to be detected and studied more fully. In a well-developed model it should be possible to go beyond mere detection to reach some assessment of the sensitivity of sales or profits to changes in the factors, and to indicate those values of the variables likely to lead to maximum benefit.

For most companies, this situation is likely still to lie some way in the future, but the benefits in terms of being able to plan confirmatory experiments – or experiments within a limited range of the independent variables as opposed to feeling one's way through a series of exploratory operations – will be clear.

Better pre-testing methods

Alternative developments that could have similar effects when dealing with innovations, as opposed to changes in the degree of effort, may come from a more specific linkage between the results of the various pre-testing stages on products, advertisements, packs, etc., and the likely effects on sales or profits. At present, the various forms of pre-testing are taken very much on faith and no scientific assessment of their validity is possible since few of those innovations which fail at a pre-testing stage reach the market. The fact that an acceptable proportion of the innovations 'passing' the pre-testing stages do succeed is not in itself sufficient evidence of the validity of the procedures unless we can present similar evidence to show that a high proportion of rejects fail. However, this faith is probably not misplaced. What does need to be done, however, and which would be invaluable in all forms of pre-testing, is to establish a connection between pre-test scores and the effect of an innovation on sales, or else on an intermediate measure such as awareness or image which could itself be used to project these changes.

This forms very much a long-term development, far more difficult in some areas than in others. There would, however, appear to be scope for a manufacturer, as, for example, a publisher of part-works who is already launching a succession of new and similar products, to develop a standardized method of pre-testing his products that could provide a useful correlation between pre-test scores and actual sales as an aid to prediction. This would then enable the expected outcome of any experimental launch to be more closely specified and early results examined more fruitfully for indications of whether predictions were being achieved.

Mini-testing

A more immediate development already taking place is the 'mini-test' involving the use of some form of a captive panel of consumers. This is another attempt to bridge the gap between the pre-testing stages and the use of a full-scale marketing experiment with all its risks and problems.

The basic idea is for a panel of consumers to be formed, who then agree, or are induced, to make a significant proportion of their purchases in the fields being covered from a particular source. The source may be a warehouse from which consumers order by telephone and from which the goods are delivered; it may be a mobile shop which follows a consistent route and calls on the same people week by week; or it may be a door-to-door salesman using a van simply as a stockroom from which he can make immediate delivery. Where a mobile shop is not used, the consumers are informed of the range of products available from the source through a magazine/catalogue issued at regular, fairly frequent, intervals of perhaps every four weeks. It therefore becomes possible to introduce into the system new products, new flavours, colours, packs, offers of various types, or to introduce into the magazine new advertising copy. The precise details of what can be included and what can be done vary with the specific type of operation and the way it is set up.

The research results are tabulated from records of purchases made from the source of the various brands, packs, etc., by individual panel members, though some existing operations also arrange to collect members' purchases from other sources through a normal type of diary operation.

While some remarkably good projections to the levels achieved in wider markets have been obtained from such panels, the conditions under which the experiments are carried out are not those in which enough of the factors operating in the wider market can generally be introduced for the experiments to become adequate substitutes for projectable test-launching or market testing, where the risks inherent in the situation call for them. On the other hand, this can be a highly valuable technique for securing additional information beyond the pre-testing stage, involving, as it does, the vital marketing factor of paying money for goods and as an aid to assessing whether the risks of a wider marketing experiment should be undertaken. This method has the additional advantage that, although the experiment is being carried out among the consuming public, the results can only be measured by the research company operating the facility and will be available only to the manufacturer commissioning the research.

In continuation of this theme, there would appear to be a slight but growing tendency for companies in appropriate situations to operate small experimental launches in fairly restricted areas so as to gain more information on the likely success of a product before becoming involved in a full-scale experimental launch. This, of course, is time-consuming but where a manufacturer is contemplating marketing a radically new product springing from a major technological break-through, he may have a sufficient lead to allow these additional stages while faced with a risk situation that justifies sacrificing some of that lead time so as to avoid the risk of the heavy costs that could be incurred by an abortive test-launch.

Controlled experimental conditions

The third area, concerning the exogenous variables, is among the most interesting and may be developed in at least two ways: (a) through the exercise of positive control over some at least of the exogenous variables, and (b) through the development or adaptation of facilities permitting two or more side-by-side experiments, or an experiment with its control, to be mounted in the same geographic area.

The first of these developments is already offered by a number of research companies who have established facilities for running experiments with control over distribution in selected areas. It may involve warehousing, delivery, and shelf-filling to maintain in-stock distribution at a constant high level for the product concerned, as well as organizing and servicing any such anciliary factors as displays, promotional material, literature, etc., associated with the experiment. Thus, where distribution is an exogenous and not an independent variable, any adverse effects from a failure to achieve a desired minimum level, or from variations occurring during the course of the experiment, can be avoided. This is often the situation that happens where experiments aim at assessing the repurchase patterns of triers of a new product, or at measuring the effects of changes in pack or price, the use of special offers or other promotions, changes in advertising or media, and similar exercises, while keeping measurements free from any effects due to variations in distribution.

Exogenous variables like price or display can often be controlled for the duration of an experiment by agreement between store operators and the research organization, but others, like those involving competitive advertising or promotions, may never become amenable to control, though tentative discussions have been held in at least one British industry with a view to mounting jointly controlled and financed experiments in areas of common interest.

Experiment and control in a single area

To provide some measure of the effects of the exogenous variables on the dependent variable during the course of an experiment, a control operation is usually organized simultaneously in a similar area. The thinking behind this, applicable also to side-by-side testing of two or more alternative changes, is based on the assumption that these exogenous variables will behave similarly and produce similar effects in separate areas, but this, of course, is liable to turn out differently. Competitive activity, strikes, weather, and other factors may produce differences between areas that will interfere with interpretations, while changes between the areas due to exogenous variables can obscure the changes due to different treatments.

Using a number of different areas, for the experiment as well as for control purposes, will enable a more precise assessment to be made of the significance of any observed changes, but another solution here is to mount the experiment and control operation within the same geographic boundaries. This is often done in some experiments, when test and control stores for pack or display tests may be drawn from the same towns, or coupons or samples distributed within different streets in the same town.

The extension of this method to experiments on advertising through press or television is a comparatively recent development that enables different campaigns or schedules to be assessed against each other or against the results from control panels, each panel or sample of respondents being subject to the same general environment, the same stores, the same competitive activity, the same strikes, and so forth. These developments have been carried farthest in the United States with such facilities as the Milwaukee Ad-Lab and with Community Antenna Television. Both the Ad-Lab and CAT-V permit different advertising to be presented to balanced samples of consumers within a single environment, thus making experiments subject so far as possible to the same exogenous variables.

The Ad-Lab

The Milwaukee Ad-Lab was originally set up in 1960 by the *Milwaukee Journal*, and it provided facilities for split-running press advertising with a complex circulation system intended to give balanced coverage to each alternative version within the total distribution area. Samples of the population receiving each version were recruited to normal consumer diary panels to provide a means of measuring any differences or changes in purchasing patterns among those exposed to the different campaigns. Thus the effect of the exogenous variables was made as similar as possible between the experimental groups and the control, and they were virtually eliminated from any comparisons between results.

At a later stage, in 1964, television was added to the Ad-Lab's facilities. The problems here were more complex, since households were free to switch between a number of stations covering the area, the mere restriction of different commercials to different channels not providing any control over reception. Neither was it feasible, nor would it have met experimental requirements, to split the transmissions from stations to permit different commercials to be broadcast on the same channel to different parts of the area. The solution was, in many senses, a negative one, but it is still one that affords a means of mounting experiments and controls in a single context. The TV sets of the consumer panel members are fitted with 'muters' which are controlled from a transmitter and which cut off both vision and sound when a coded signal is received and restore it instantaneously when the reverse instruction is received by the muter. In this way it is possible to broadcast two campaigns, A and B, to two panels of households, X and Y, so that members of panel X will not normally see campaign B, and members of panel Y will not normally see campaign A. Any differences which develop between the purchasing patterns of the two panels can therefore be attributed more certainly to the different campaigns than would be the case if different areas with different exogenous factors had been involved.

The method is attractive when testing different campaigns, or when testing different levels of advertising pressure, but there still remain a number of aspects that fall short of the ideal. First, there is the fact that, to screen two campaigns, two complete schedules have to be booked. The cost of this is probably insignificant, but a number of factors germane to an experimental situation arise. If the campaigns are booked on different stations, then the self-selection process through which people tune to different stations may lead to the two campaigns being shown to audiences with different characteristics that may be reflected in purchasing patterns. If, as normally happens, the two campaigns are booked through the same stations, then clearly they cannot have identical schedules – the members of panel X being exposed to campaign A at different times from those when panel Y is being exposed to campaign B. In the long run, it would be possible to rotate the schedules so that, so far as possible, the two sets of timings are restored to parity, but there is an additional and possibly more serious problem that must be kept in mind.

To provide the two research panels with the necessary opportunities to see the two campaigns, the total weight of transmitted advertising is doubled, and this double weight is received by the majority of the viewing population in the area apart from the minority on the panels whose sets are fitted with muters. Thus, while the two panels are being subjected to identical exogenous factors in an effort to improve the efficiency of the experiment, the exogenous factors related to the weight of advertising received by the surrounding population are themselves being changed in ways that would not pertain if either campaign were being used normally in a wider area. Whether or not this will have any effect in a particular experiment is an open question, but there would appear to be at least some possibility that changes could be produced in other exogenous variables that, while still operating equally on both research panels, would leave any observed differences open to some doubt. For example, the doubled weight of advertising broadcast to the majority of the population could have effects on their purchasing leading, more or less directly, to a wider distribution of the product, greater in-store activity, more word-of-mouth comment, or other phenomena that could so change the purchasing patterns of both panels that the small effects due to the different campaigns would be swamped.

Despite these criticisms of the method, there is no doubt that the use of muters in conjunction with consumer panels does offer facilities for some types of experiment that are a considerable advance on using different geographic areas for experiments and control operations. The main reasons for raising these criticisms are so that the limitations should be appreciated by those who are contemplating using the method and because they appear to be avoided by the CAT-V method.

Community Antenna TV

The CAT-V method needs a community that obtains its television signals via a single main antenna, from which they are carried by wire, boosted as necessary, to individual receivers. Switchgear and a type of 'transmitter' are then introduced into the system so that commercials being broadcast from the parent station can be prevented from reaching a proportion of the receivers, other commercials being substituted in their place. The method has developed rapidly in the United States, first through the modification of existing CAT-V systems, so that receivers in particular areas could be isolated, but more recently through its incorporation into new facilities at their inception, with the added refinement of the installation of split-cables. These virtually permit the transmission of different commercials to alternate households throughout the community, and have the potential of providing experimental and control panels that are subjected to identical exogenous conditions.

Apart from overcoming the problems inherent in the muter system, the CAT-V method has an added advantage in that recruitment to a panel to fit special equipment to a TV set is not needed and the experimental commercials can be transmitted to large numbers of households. There will therefore exist adequate numbers of respondents available for *ad hoc* surveys into awareness, recall, comprehension, etc., without any interference with the viability of consumer purchasing panels that may be operating being necessary. This opens up the possibility of using the system to make quick assessments of new or experimental commercials or campaigns, through twenty-four-hour recall or similar methods, prior to use in a wider area.

A further development is the linking of 'mini-test' facilities for distributing new or changed products, with highly localized transmission of TV commercials over a limited cable area. This brings TV advertising within the operation of a mini-test and greatly increases its potential value.

Neither the muter type of operation nor CAT-V facilities are yet (1970) available in Great Britain. Attempts to launch a muter service have been made, but have not yet succeeded, either because of the high costs involved in setting up the facility and the necessary research panels, or because of organizational problems. Community antenna methods have not been developed here, partly because of legal requirements that prevent any alteration to a signal between the antenna and the receivers which it serves, and partly because the use of such antennae is as yet far more limited than in the United States. Whether the switch from VHF to UHF will lead to larger communities being dependent on such aerials in Britain, and whether legal and other obstacles to their being used for research purposes can be overcome, remains to be seen.

The use of overlap areas

One method of running an advertising experiment and its control in a single area, or of running two experiments side-by-side, is to use an overlap area in which two local media are received. This has been used in Great Britain for television advertising by taking part of an overlap area between two stations and running a different campaign in each of them. Although the whole of each area then receives its respective transmissions, measurements are restricted to panels or surveys among residents in the overlap area, who are stratified according to the station which they receive. To be fully effective in providing the same exogenous conditions for each sample, it is necessary for competitive advertising on each of the two stations to be the same in content, weight and scheduling, and while this condition may frequently be fulfilled, it certainly cannot be assumed, and prior analysis of published data is vital.

It is not, of course, possible to get the close intermingling of samples possible with CAT-V, since reception of the two stations depends largely on the local geography, and homes receiving one station or the other will tend to be clustered. Where the clusters are large, with whole neighbourhoods tuned to the same station, the two audiences may no longer be subject to the same shopping conditions, or other factors, and there may be considerable differences in the occupational or social class patterns between the two that may create difficulties in obtaining balanced research samples.

The members of the samples used should, of course, be exposed to the same competition from other television stations, which may vary in Great Britain since ITV and BBC coverage is not uniform, and there may also be conditions of multiple overlap where the audiences of each of the commercial stations may divide into further groups depending on which BBC station they receive. This situation is likely to become more complex as UHF is developed.

The overlap area method has some potential as a testing mechanism to enable side-by-side testing or experiment and control to take place within one area, but there are a number of problems that may reduce the extent to which the two audiences are, in fact, subject to identical extraneous conditions. If use is considered for any form of projectable experiment, there should first be a rigorous examination of past advertising in the market on the two stations, as well as of the patterns of reception within the area, so as to ensure that some of the benefits of using a single area will remain and that the operation will not degenerate into, in effect, a two-area test within one small part of the country.

The figures in Table 12.1 were taken from past data and show how the pattern of commercials for two brands differed widely between two 'overlapping' transmitters. Tests of campaigns for a brand c could be seriously affected by these differences in competitive activity.

Figure 12.1 Numbers of 30-second spots in overlap area

| | Transmitter 1 | | Transmitter 2 | |
	Brand A	Brand B	Brand A	Brand B
week 1	8	9	5	6
2	8	6	6	25
3	9	7	10	8
4		9		6
weeks 1-4	25	31	21	45
5		17	2	5
6	9	7	14	4
7	11	9	8	5
8	10	8	5	2
weeks 5-8	30	41	29	16
9	6	14	6	7
10		8	4	5
11	3	11	2	4
12	8	8	5	5
13	8	9	2	9
weeks 9-13	25	50	19	30
total	80	122	69	91

The long-term prospect

In the long run, marketing experiments are likely to be influenced by two main factors: increased control over the experimental situation, and increased knowledge of markets and how they operate. The first should lead to greater precision in the results, possibly with the aid of more sophisticated methods of analysis and hopefully through wider use of multi-area experiments. The second should lead to a more precise specification in advance of the expected outcome of an experiment, thus providing opportunities for the better planning and measurement of experiments, and thence to a more successful projection or prediction of the results to be expected in a wider market.

A greater understanding of markets, with the development of models of at least some parts of some markets, may eventually enable firm predictions to be made, so that in certain cases experiments will no longer be needed. On the other hand, the need to fill gaps in models which cannot be closed by the analysis of past data, and the need to validate models before they can safely be used for prediction, may lead to an increase in experimentation. Either way, there will remain many areas concerned with the product itself, packaging, advertising content, and other 'creative' areas, where the variable cannot be scaled and where testing in the market will for a long time to come remain the only practicable method for obtaining solid advance information of the effect on profits to be expected from an introduction into the wider market.

Further reading

Chapter 1

ACHENBAUM, A A *The Purpose of Test Marketing* Proceedings of the 47th National Conference, American Marketing Association, 1964.

WILLS, G and HAYHURST, R *Test Marketing: How Can We Imprcve Practice* 12th Annual Conference papers, Market Research Society, 1969.

Chapter 2

FISHER, R A *The Design of Experiments* Chapters 1–3, Oliver & Boyd 1935.

Chapter 3

GREEN, P E and FRANK, R E Bayesian statistics and marketing research *Journal of the Royal Statistical Society*, Series C, **XV** 3, November 1966.

GREEN, P E and TULL, D S *Research for Marketing Decisions* Prentice-Hall 1966.

MONTGOMERY, D B and URBAN, G L *Management Science in Marketing* Prentice-Hall 1969.

SCHLAIFER, R *Probability and Statistics for Business Decisions* McGraw-Hill 1959.

Chapter 6

APPEL, V Multi-market testing: A practical method for choosing between media alternatives *Commentary* (Journal of the Market Research Society), **VII** 2, April 1965.

BANKS, S *Experimentation in Marketing* McGraw-Hill 1965.

BUZZELL, R D *Mathematical Models and Marketing Management* Harvard University Press 1965.

Chapter 7

CHRISTOPHER, M *A cluster analysis of towns in England and Wales according to their suitability for test market locations* University of Bradford Management Centre 1969.

GREEN, P E, FRANK, R E and ROBINSON, P J Cluster analysis in test market selection *Management Science* **13**, 8, April 1967.

Chapter 8

MOSER, C A *Survey Methods in Social Investigation* Heinemann 1958.

PARTEN, M *Surveys, Polls and Samples: Practical Procedures* Harper & Row 1950.

Chapter 9

BAUM, J and DENNIS, K E R *The estimation of the expected brand share of a new product* ESOMAR Congress 1961.

CHATFIELD, C, EHRENBERG, A S C and GOODHARDT, G J Progress in a simplified model of stationary purchasing behaviour *Journal of the Royal Statistical Society* Series A **124**, 317–67, 1966.

CROXTON, F E, COWDEN, D J and KLEIN, S *Applied General Statistics* Pitman 3rd edn 1968.

KISH, L *Survey Sampling* Wiley 1965.

MORONEY, M J *Facts From Figures* Penguin Books 1965

PARFITT, J H and COLLINS, B J K The use of consumer panels for brand-share prediction *Journal of Marketing Research*, **V**, 2 May 1968.

Chapter 10

DAVIS, E J Test marketing: an examination of sales patterns found during forty-four recent tests. In *Research in Marketing* 7th Annual Conference papers, Market Research Society 1964.

GOLD, J A Testing test market predictions *Journal of Marketing Research*, **1**, August 1964.

Index